magical
beasts

magical
beasts

Their powers, their contribution
and how to call for their help

marie bruce

quantum

LONDON • NEW YORK • TORONTO • SYDNEY

quantum

An imprint of W. Foulsham and Co. Ltd
The Publishing House, Bennetts Close, Cippenham, Slough,
Berkshire, SL1 5AP, England

ISBN 0-572-02928-4

Printed in Great Britain by Creative Print & Design (Wales), Ebbw Vale.

Contents

This book is dedicated to my grandmother, Ada, who passed from this life on the Winter Solstice 2002 – a true Queen Bee if ever there was one! May her spirit soar.

It is also for Pepe – I will never forget you – and for Pyewackett, my faithful friend and familiar, who always makes me laugh and keeps me sane through the dark days.

Introduction

Animals have always been a part of magic. From the totem animals of Native Americans to the beasts depicted on hereditary coats of arms, they have been invoked down the ages by humans as a powerful source of help and support.

Magical Beasts will show you how to harness the power of animals for yourself. Using the concepts of thought forms, power animals, spell-casting, visualisation and traditional pets, this book will provide you with a key to the secrets of animal magic.

Call upon the hoarding instincts of the squirrel to help you with your finances, ask the dove to bring you love, or invite the courage and cunning of the wolf to help you through a difficult time. Invoke a dragon of protection, fly a winged horse on an astral journey, attune with the masculine spirit of paganism through the mighty stag, seek answers from the sphinx or healing from the dolphin. Get to know your own pet in a completely new way, seeing it as a magical familiar and a source of gentle power that will enhance your spell-castings.

Our world and our imaginations are filled with magical beasts. Only when we have learnt to respect them fully and accept them as equals can we gain a true understanding of their power. This book will help you to do just that.

I hope that you enjoy your magical walk with beasts!

Blessed be!

Morgana

The Ark of Magic

This book will teach you how to harness the age-old magic of familiars and power animals. For most people the term 'familiar' conjures up images of a stereotypical witch whispering secrets and spells into the ears of a coal-black cat. But animal magic is not confined to witches and witchcraft, and the powers of beasts have been put to good use across the globe and throughout the centuries. It is also true that animals have suffered great cruelty in the name of witchcraft. We have only to think of the cats that were tortured and killed alongside their mistresses during the Burning Times (the era of persecution of witches in Europe) to know that this is true.

This book, however, was written with the welfare of animals in mind at all times. You will find no spells here to harm or mistreat any living creature. That is not the Wiccan way. I have also deliberately avoided using old-fashioned terms such as 'wing of bat' and 'tongue of dog'. These phrases are well known from Shakespeare's *Macbeth*, in which they are used by the three witches. They are actually old country terms for specific herbs and do not refer to any particular animal or animal part, but they can be misinterpreted, leading to confusion and cruelty, so they have no place within these pages.

It has been a long-standing joke in my family that I think more of animals than I do of people, and there could be said to be a grain of truth in that! I appreciate the total loyalty and unconditional love that animals can give, and noticed at an early age that these traits are often found wanting in humans! I have always been an animal lover and have lavished affection on my pets since earliest childhood. When I was a little girl, my wild and foundling 'pets' included a bright green caterpillar called Freddy, a fledgling sparrow called Bobby, a small black kitten with an injured paw, and a frog I found at a local pond and decided to take home, convinced that he was really a prince!

In addition, my brother and I gained a more conventional collection of pond loaches, goldfish, hamsters, guinea pigs, mice, budgies, dogs and, at one time, a pony called Misty. If you can relate to any of this, if you have a deep-seated love of all animals and would like to use their powers to improve your life, then this is definitely the book for you!

What is a familiar?

One of the most common terms associated with animals and magic is 'familiar'. A familiar is a magical working companion, a creature that lends its energies to yours for protection, meditational guidance, inspiration, and spell-casting, and for better understanding of and communication with a particular species. Familiars can also help us to overcome fear of a certain creature. And they are not as elusive as people seem to think. If you take a look around any town or city you will see familiars everywhere – carved into the stonework of old buildings; pictured on bill boards, posters and heraldic shields; playing with children in gardens and parks; represented in the logos of large companies; adopted as mascots for sports teams ... and so on.

The magic of animals is a natural part of the universal power, and humankind has always tapped into this source of strength. Today, most people do this on an entirely unconscious level. They may have an interest in a particular species or be drawn repeatedly to one type of pet, without really knowing why. These people are responding to the call of a familiar. Perhaps, as you read these words, you automatically know who your familiar is; perhaps you need to study a little further and delve a little deeper before you recognise it. But one thing is certain, if you were drawn to read this book, then your familiar is trying to tell you something.

One of the wonderful things about animal magic is that it is largely visionary. Yes, there are some tools required, but, in essence, your work with familiars can take place entirely in your head if you want it to. This means that it is effectively one of the most accessible forms of magic around, and is very transportable and discreet! You can call on your familiar while cooking dinner, driving to work, standing in the supermarket queue, giving a presentation, relaxing in a hot bath, sitting on a bus or attending an important appointment. There really are no limits in this work, and if made with love and respect, your call will be answered.

Animal magic is available to anyone, whatever their age, gender or level of magical experience and ability, because the animal kingdom touches us all in some way. We all have a favourite animal, bird or insect – a creature that calls to us, that we feel we can relate to in some way. And those of you who consider yourselves to be animal lovers probably have a whole variety of favourites to choose from. I know I do.

Making contact with a familiar

So how do you make contact with a familiar? To answer this question we need to look briefly at the world of metaphysics. In metaphysics it is generally believed that there are several planes of existence. The two that concern us here are the physical plane and the astral plane. The physical plane is, of course, our own realm of existence, the Earth. The astral plane is a realm of existence that cannot be seen with the physical eye but only with the mind's eye, or third eye as it is also known. This is the realm of visualisations, meditations, imaginings, dreams (both nocturnal dreams and daydreams) and the initial stages of magic and spell-castings.

Nothing can manifest on the physical plane unless it has first been 'seen' on the astral plane. In other words, in order for the computer to be invented, it first had to be envisioned by someone. The computer therefore existed first on the astral plane. In working magic, this process is especially important – the witch or practitioner must clearly visualise the positive outcome of the spell throughout the casting. If this is done successfully, the desired result will manifest on the astral plane and then on the physical plane. If all this sounds complicated, don't worry. Visiting the astral plane is something we all do quite naturally, and there are ways in which we can become more aware of doing this. If you ever had an imaginary friend as a child, you were actually interacting with a being from the astral realms.

Because many of the spells and exercises in this book involve connecting with the astral plane, or shadow world as it is also called, it is vital that you should feel comfortable when making this link. This is not, in fact, a new skill that you have to learn, but something you already do all the time. For instance, when you begin to feel hunger pangs you immediately start to think about what you'd like for lunch. By visualising your lunch – let's say it's a pizza – you have already created its existence on the astral plane. The act of going to a pizza parlour and buying the pizza creates the link between astral realm and the physical realm, and within minutes you're tucking in and enjoying your lunch.

Here's another example of connecting with the shadow world. Have you ever wanted to have a lovely dream about your favourite pop star or actor – your own personal heart-throb? If so, you probably found yourself thinking about that person more than usual, maybe watching their movies or music videos more regularly. And what often happens? You end up having some fabulous sexy dreams! (Don't be shy – we've all had them!) But note how the situation here is reversed. In this example, we work on the physical plane first, by listening to music and watching videos, and then we connect with the astral by experiencing the dream. So you can see that the connection will work both ways and in both directions.

When it comes to animal magic, however, there are times when you link with the astral realm but don't connect it to the physical plane – it's fine to love tigers and to work with them on the astral plane as familiars, but you really wouldn't want to bring one into your physical existence! Which leads us to another subject.

Types of familiar

Familiars, power animals, totems – what are the differences and what are the similarities? Well, the short answer is, they are all the same; these are just different terms used by different groups of people to express the same thing: an animal with whose magical powers we have a connection. 'Totem' is the Native American term, 'power animal' the Celtic term, and 'familiar' the term used in British witchcraft. The three terms can be used interchangeably and you can use whichever one you feel most comfortable with. I personally prefer 'familiar' and 'power animal', as I have a British/Celtic heritage, and these are the words I have largely used throughout this book. However, if you prefer to use the word 'totem' or some other word that is native to your background, then please do so. Never let a strange word stop you from making magic – just substitute for it a word you're more comfortable with.

Just as there are different types of magic, there are different types of familiar. Some reside only in the astral realms, while others flit between our world and the shadow world beyond.

Pets

When most people hear the word 'familiar', they think of a pet that has a close connection to its human. You'll notice that I didn't use the terms 'master' or 'mistress'. This is because animals can never be owned. If anything, most animals are freer spirits than we are, and it is very disrespectful to view them as a possession or a commodity. I also detest the term 'livestock', as it places our fellow creatures in a position of inferiority. But this is just one of my personal soap boxes! You are free to disagree – and I'm sure every farmer in the land will! Not all pets are familiars, but all have the potential to become so. A pet who is also a familiar will have a deep loyalty and affection for its human companion. There is usually some form of psychic link and the love shared is totally unconditional on both sides. This type of familiar generally shares our home or is stabled or housed nearby. It is part of the physical plane, although true familiars of this sort can communicate with us through our dreams, and so they have a place in the shadow world too. We will be looking in more depth at pets as familiars in Chapter 3 (see page 33).

Dangerous liaisons

Another kind of familiar is a part of the physical plane, but for some reason we cannot bring it into our lives as a pet. This is usually because it would be dangerous or impractical to do so. Power animals of this variety include lions, tigers, dolphins, whales, wolves, bears, gorillas and elephants. Witches who feel a connection with such animals, and many do, will work with them on the astral plane through spell-casting and meditation, and will also bring the essence of their power animal into their environment using pictures, shrines, statues and so on.

Perhaps the only way to have these creatures in your physical world is to work with them professionally – by becoming a marine biologist or a zoo keeper for example. If this isn't possible, try to take regular trips to safari parks and conservation zoos. Needless to say, you should only support those establishments where the animals are treated with love and respect and given the best of care and attention.

Enter the realms of fantasy ...

The third kind of familiar is the mythological beast. Here we are talking dragons (very popular), unicorns, winged horses, griffins, basilisks, phoenixes, winged bulls, gargoyles and other such creatures. In magical terms, it is said that such creatures once lived in our world but, for reasons known only to themselves, withdrew and now exist solely in the astral realm. Does this mean that they are not real? Absolutely not. Many things that we cannot see – such as joy, love and despair – are nonetheless real and have a profound effect on our lives. Mythical creatures can be contacted via meditation, dreams, visualisations and thought forms. Their energies are very real and can be felt in our lives if we open ourselves up to them. And once you've made friends with a dragon, you will never be left unprotected!

It has to be said, though, that of all the familiars we have looked at so far, mythical creatures can be the most elusive and the most difficult to contact. Unless, that is, they have some reason for wanting to contact you. In this case they may make the first move, and you may see them in dreams or find them coming into your life via TV and movies, or perhaps the gift of an appropriate figurine. We will look more closely at various mythical creatures in Chapters 12 and 13 and will be visiting them throughout the course of this book.

Shape-shifting

Shape-shifting – the very words evoke feelings of magic and excitement! But is shape-shifting real or is it only an aspect of fiction and film? Well, it's both actually. Shape-shifting is the magical ability to become something else: for a human to transform into a bird, an animal or even a tree. This concept has fascinated the human mind for centuries, to such an extent that shape-shifting is a huge part of folklore and has moved into the realms of children's fiction, TV, music videos and blockbuster movies.

The mostly widely known aspect of shape-shifting is the werewolf legend, closely followed by the historical belief that witches could magically transform themselves into cats and hares in order to escape their inquisitors. A more subtle example of the shape-shifting phenomenon occurs in the vampire legend, in which the un-dead transform themselves into bats, and instances can be seen in fairy tales such as *Cinderella, Beauty and the Beast* and *The Frog Prince*. Turning to the world of TV, instances of shape-shifting have been included in episodes of *Charmed, Buffy the Vampire Slayer, The X-Files* and *Sabrina the Teenage Witch*, to name but a few. In children's fiction, shape-shifting occurs in books such as *The Box of Delights, The Magician's House* and, of course, the *Harry Potter* series. TV and film adaptations of all these books give wonderful interpretations of how shape-shifting might work, using animation and computer graphics. But by far the best example of TV shape-shifting, and my personal favourite, can be seen in the music video of A-HA's 'Hunting High and Low'. Here, the band members are magically transformed into a lion, an eagle and a shark, exploring the three realms of land, air and sea in order to search for a lost love.

What all these examples demonstrate is that shape-shifting has taken a strong hold on the human psyche; and, as with most legends and myths, the concept has its roots set firmly in reality. Shape-shifting originated among ancient shamanic tribes. Whether the shaman was called a witch doctor, a high priest, a witch, a medicine man or a high priestess, most cultures and communities had a wise woman or a cunning man who would cast spells, throw charms, and commune with elementals and astral entities for the good of their people.

Part of the shaman's job was to connect with the animal kingdom. Initially this was in order to magically ensure success during hunting, and also to offer thanks to the creatures whose lives would be sacrificed for the continuation of the tribe. To aid him in this connection, the shaman would often wear skins, masks and head gear made from the hide of the animal he was trying to connect with. Circle dances, drumming and chanting were employed to raise magical power, and meditational states were achieved to complete the process of animal communication. It was during this meditation that the wisdom of the animal would be spoken through the mouth of the shaman – giving the impression that he had, on some level, shape-shifted into the animal in question.

With the passage of time this type of animal magic was developed, expanded and used for a number of purposes. Speed and stamina during a journey, increased strength, courage in battle, heightened vision and various other qualities would be invoked by calling upon the relevant animal and 'worn' by shamans and tribe members alike. In this way, people gained some control over their lives and the environment in which they lived. Before long, warriors were being named after their animal counterparts. Tribes and clans often took a particular creature to be their own guardian power animal and would associate only with other clans whose power animal was compatible with their own. This is still the case with some Native American tribes. For today's witches and practitioners of animal magic, shape-shifting takes place during the act of meditation. Instead of simply visualising a particular creature, in order to shape-shift the witch will connect with the mind of the creature, and will then go on a meditational journey, seeing the world through the eyes of her chosen animal. During this journey, she will try to be aware of the sights, sounds, scents and sensations that she comes across in her new shape-shifted state, thus fully experiencing the life and challenges faced by that particular creature.

During meditations of this kind, the practitioner may come across situations and challenges that reflect a current problem in the real world; thus shape-shifting can work as a problem solver by teaching skills of survival crucial in the animal kingdom. Although shape-shifting meditations are an advanced technique, they are perfectly safe to perform – remember that this is an astral journey and no harm can come to you. And if you practise regularly, you will find that your shape-shifting journeys become clearer and more detailed.

Shape–shifting Visualisation Spell

What you need

A pile of cushions, incense and meditation music (optional)

What you do

⭐ Make sure that you are in a quiet place and will not be disturbed. If you like, you can have incense burning and meditation music playing in the background. Pile the cushions on the floor and lie down, with your spine straight. Close your eyes and take three deep breaths. Now concentrate on relaxing each part of your body, beginning at your feet and working upwards. Once you are completely relaxed, begin the simple meditation below.

⭐ In your mind's eye you are walking through a beautiful forest. Up ahead you can see a clearing in the trees and something sparkling in the sunlight. You make your way to the clearing and notice a beautiful full-length mirror, crafted in gold and silver and shining brightly in the summer sun. Walking towards the mirror you notice that instead of reflecting the forest and the trees, the mirror shows thick, swirling mists. You step closer to the mirror and as you do so, the mists clear and you see the image of an animal gazing at you intently. This creature has something to teach you. It is the creature you can learn the most from at this point in your life, yet it may not be the one you expected to see. To connect and shape-shift into this animal, simply step into the magic mirror. Allow the meditation to take over now and let your consciousness go where it will. You are the creature of the mirror and you can see, hear and scent things as he would. Observe what challenges you come across and how you deal with them in your animal state, as these are the lessons you are here to learn.

⭐ Once you have completed your journey, return to the mirror and shape-shift into your human form by stepping back through the miror. Walk away from the clearing in the woods and as you do so, feel yourself becoming more aware of your true surroundings. Open your eyes and make a note of your meditation in your book of Earth Shadows (see page 29).

Shape-shifting is only one way to work with animal energies. If it does not appeal to you, there are plenty of other ways to bring magical beasts into your life. We will be experimenting with some of them in the following chapters, so read on ...

Earth Child

I n this chapter we will be looking at what it takes to be an earth child and a practitioner of animal magic. Animals live close to the earth and are fully in tune with the natural cycles of the seasons, so it stands to reason that if we are to communicate well with our fellow creatures, we too should make every effort to become closer to nature and the world around us. Too many people are so wrapped up in the daily grind of making a living, paying the bills, bringing up children and cleaning the house that they rarely stop for a moment to look around them. Think for a second: when was the last time you truly enjoyed the sight of a rainbow? Or the feel of the wind in your hair, the rain on your skin? When did you last walk in your garden barefoot, or drink in the fragrance of spring blossom and summer roses? When did you last make time to go out at night just to enjoy the beauty of the stars and the moonlight? Do you feel excited by the first snowfall of winter, or do you get grumpy because you'll have to spend ten minutes clearing it off your car?

Nature is all around us, even if we live in the midst of a large city. There are stars, clouds, trees, flowers, rainfalls, thunder and lightning, snow and frost, sunshine, rainbows, full moons ... Wherever you are, wherever you live, the magic of nature is all around you. If your life revolves around simply getting through the day, you are neglecting the deeper part of yourself. Everyone deserves a little 'me time'; it is vital to our mental health and well-being, and if you neglect yourself in this way, you will soon find that you are feeling stressed and frazzled and that life seems to be a constant uphill struggle. Getting back in touch with nature can help you to release the stresses of the day and will leave you feeling calm, centred and ready to take on the challenges of life. And to be an effective practitioner of animal magic you must be calm, free of stress and in tune with the natural environment around you. So let's begin with a little awareness exercise ...

Earth child awareness

This exercise can be adapted to suit your lifestyle and to fit in with family commitments and so on. It will take five days to complete, but these days do not have to run consecutively, so you could use one of your days off each week and spread the exercise over a period of five weeks. If you simply cannot devote a whole day to your magic, then spend as much time as is practical for you on this process – though you should devote a minimum of two consecutive hours to each of the stages. Only then will you reap the full rewards. You will also need to keep a note book and pencil with you during the time you spend on this exercise, so that you can write down your experiences, thoughts, feelings, fears and so on.

Animals depend on their senses for survival, and because of this their senses are very acute. This exercise is designed to help you to fully experience each one of your own senses and to become more aware of them in general. You will find that heightened senses are of great value in animal magic and meditations.

For all of these exercises you will need to spend some time in nature – perhaps walking in the park or a wood, or simply pottering around in the garden.

Day one: sight

Take your note book and write the word 'sight' at the top of the page. Now go out into nature and become fully aware of your sense of sight. Acknowledge all that you see. Pay heed to the weather – is it sunny, rainy, misty, clear or dull? How does the light affect the way things look? Take a look at the trees. Can you see any unusual patterns, shapes or faces within the bark or the leaves? What wildlife do you see? What colour is the sky? What colour is the earth beneath your feet? Do the cloud formations look like anything in particular? Are there any flowers or herbs around you? Are the trees black and bare or are they in leaf? What colour and shape are the leaves? Make a note of all that you see, all that your eyes are telling you. Write down not only what you see but also how you feel about what you see.

Now try to see the same view from a different perspective by standing on a bench or lying flat on the ground. Do things look different from this angle? Once again, write down your thoughts and feelings. Most especially, be sure to make a note of all the animals you come across. They may give you a hint as to who your familiar is, so notice their appearance and behaviour.

When you are back indoors again, continue to be aware of the sights around you.

Day two: sound

Write the word 'sound' at the top of a clean page of your note book and once again go out into nature. For the first stage of this process, while you are actually listening, you should keep your eyes closed. You may find that it helps to wear a sleep mask over your eyes during this part of the exercise. If you like, you can record your thoughts and feelings on a tape recorder and transfer them to your note book once you have completed the exercise. If you choose not to make a recording, wait until you have fully absorbed the sounds around you before you open your eyes and start to write.

Close your eyes and become aware of all that you can hear. What do you hear right now? Are birds singing? Can you recognise which species? Can you tell the difference between the bark of a dog and the bark of a fox? Do you hear the wind howling, or is it blowing gently? Are there leaves rustling, children playing? Do you hear any small creatures moving about in the hedgerows? Once again, record all that you can hear, as well as your thoughts and feelings about it.

Now repeat the process while covering your right ear with your hand. What are the differences? Next, do the same thing while covering your left ear. What do you hear now? Can you tell which direction sounds are coming from? Are they behind you, above you, in the distance? Be fully open to your sense of sound.

When you are indoors again, continue to be aware of the sounds around you.

Day three: scent

Write the word 'scent' at the top of a clean page of your note book and go out into nature. Again, for the first part of this exercise, keep your eyes closed.

Scent is the most heightened sense of most animals, and yet we humans rarely give it a second thought. Today I want you to sniff everything! Drink in the various fragrances – newly mown grass, fresh rainfall, the smell of spring or the first tang of winter frost in the air. Each season has its own particular smell. What season are we in right now? What does it smell like? What do trees smell like, or the rotting leaves in autumn and winter? What does a snowy morning smell like, a sunny evening, a foggy night? What does your garden smell like? Compare the fragrance of lavender with that of a rose. How do herbs smell? Could you recognise the scent of burning sage?

When you have spent some time registering your scent impressions, describe them in your note book and note down how they make you feel. Notice what they remind you of. Is there a particular scent that always reminds you of something or someone? For instance, the fragrance of honeysuckle always makes me think of my grandmother, while the smell of car engines and garages reminds me of an old friend who worked as a mechanic. Are there any scents that unnerve you or make you fearful? Several years ago I spent some time working in a nursing home for the elderly, and I learnt that death has a fragrance all of its own, which serves as a warning that the time is very near. This may explain why animals become fearful as they are driven into an abattoir. Be open to your sense of smell and record your thoughts, feelings and associations, even the negative ones.

When you are back indoors again, continue to be aware of the smells around you.

Day four: touch

Open your note book to a new page and write the word 'touch' at the top, then go out into nature.

Today I want you to open yourself to your sense of touch. Try closing your eyes as you encounter the tactility of different objects. Notice how the sun feels on your face – or the rain. Paddle in a stream and be aware of the sensation of the water on your feet, or go for a dip in the ocean. What does that feel like? Are the waves gentle or are they crashing against your legs? Feel snow on your cheeks or a snowball in your hand. Notice the brushing of leaves against your skin. Rub your hands against tree bark. How does that feel? What is it like to walk barefoot in cool grass? To touch the petals of a rose ... or of a marigold? How does your own hair feel, or your own clothes. Which fabrics do you prefer to touch – silk, cotton, wool? Then write down your thoughts and feelings about what you have experienced.

Once you are back indoors, continue to be aware of the textures that you encounter.

Day five: taste

For the last part of this exercise, open your note book to a new page and write down the word 'taste' at the top of it. Since much of what we encounter in nature is not necessarily safe or good to eat, today you are going to exercise your awareness within your everyday life.

For the course of the day, be fully aware of the taste of everything you eat and drink. Compare chocolate with cabbage, cheese with strawberries, hot chocolate with cool white wine. Remember the strange sweets you ate as a child – candyfloss and 'space dust'! Now try to remember a completely new taste sensation, for example, your first alcoholic beverage. Perhaps there's a taste you can encounter for the first time today.

Taste doesn't just apply to food and drink, however. You can also be aware of the taste of toothpaste as you clean your teeth, a lover's kiss, the end of your pen as you chew it, your nails as you bite them, your lipstick or chapstick, salt water as you swim in the sea or chlorine in a swimming pool. Record all your taste sensations and your reactions to them.

You now have a record of all your sensory experiences over the five days. From now on, try to remain in touch with all your senses, just as animals are. This will help you to understand animals and connect with them when you begin your magical work. We humans are, after all, animals in our own right. It is important to remember this in your magical workings. When we let go of thought and experience the natural world through our five senses, we are also moving into a more magical state, so being attuned to your sensory impressions will help with your spell-castings, meditations, visualisations and so forth.

Forest friends

Another way to link with the animal kingdom is to attune with the guardian deities of all animals. In my own personal tradition – witchcraft – I call these powers the Lord of Animals and the Lady of the Woods, and I see them as aspects of the pagan god and goddess. These are the terms I have used in this book, but feel free to change them to names that fit with your own magical tradition or spiritual belief system. Choose whatever words you feel comfortable with, as a sense of the familiar will enhance your magic.

In witchcraft the Lady of the Woods is an aspect of the Great Goddess, the mother of all life and of nature in particular. She can be found in folklore, fairy tales and literature alike, and the chances are that you will have come across her at some point in your life. Snow White is one version of her – living in a woodland cottage and making friends with all the animals and elementals (i.e. dwarves) around her. In Tolkien's *The Lord of the Rings*, the Lady of the Woods is the beautiful and powerful elven queen Galadriel, while in folklore she is known as Sadb, a wild maiden with doey brown eyes, long dark tresses of untamed hair and a majestic pair of antlers growing from her brow. However you see the Lady of the Woods, she is all-powerful, and her job is to protect all wildlife from cruelty and peril.

In this task the Lady of the Woods is assisted by the Lord of Animals, known as Cernnunos, Pan and Herne the Hunter, to mention just a few of his names. In fact, Robin Hood might be considered another of them, since Robin is really a toned-down version of the Lord of Animals. This deity is generally depicted as being half man and half beast, and has a pair of horns or antlers growing from his brow. His job is to preside over the fertility of the animal kingdom and to protect all creatures as well as the Lady of the Woods with his power. Together these two nature deities are the cycle and the seed of life, and it can enhance your magic greatly to connect and attune with them in their associated environment – the woods.

Spending time in the woods can help relaxation and provide a source of great strength to those who seek it. Just a five-minute walk from my home lies an ancient bluebell wood, and I often go there to connect with nature, to gather strength and wisdom from the trees and to allow the beautiful woodland to carry away my stress and worries on the breeze. This bluebell wood was one of my favourite play areas as a child, so it has many happy associations.

I also try to visit Sherwood Forest as often as I can. Just recently, my mother and I went on a beautiful lamp-lit walk around the famous Major Oak that grows there. It was the depths of winter and very cold, and as the walk was held in the evening, in places it was pitch black. I had never seen Sherwood at night before, and it was a magical experience. Many of the more ancient oak trees were illuminated with floor lamps, shining up against the tall tree trunks, and one stretch of silver birches was lit with soft blue laser lights, making Sherwood seem suddenly like Narnia or the woods of Lothlorian! To add to the atmosphere, New Age music was playing softly through speakers hidden in the trees, and a roaring log fire was blazing in the clearing by the Major Oak itself. But it was the stillness and the quietness that really moved us – the feeling that magic was all around us, that the nature spirits were peeping at us through bare winter branches and that the enchantment of the night-time woods was creeping into our hearts, enabling us to take away a little of the magic and invoke it again and again through the power of memory.

With no summer foliage, the trees revealed their secrets to us – faces in the bark and shapes that seemed strangely familiar. My mother pointed out that part of the trunk of the Major Oak looked strikingly like an elephant's head (elephants are her power animal), while I was entranced by an ancient tree, the top of which resembled a stag rearing up on its hind legs, antlers thrown back and forelegs kicking in the air. 'That must be one of Herne's trees!' I thought to myself. The stag is one of my power animals and I often invoke Herne the Hunter in my rituals.

So, you see, much more than just a little walk, a visit to the woods can be a profoundly spiritual experience and a chance for your power animal to make contact with you. If you do have the opportunity to visit Sherwood Forest, I strongly urge you to take it. It is a truly enchanted place and anyone who is interested in magic is sure to feel its power. If this isn't practical for you, discover where your nearest wood is and try to make regular trips there. Find a quiet spot, sit still and be open to the magic of the place. Make a mental note of all the wildlife you see, especially any creatures that seem interested in you, as they could be your power animal trying to make contact. Just before you leave the wood, empty out an offering pouch of nuts, seeds and dried fruits onto the forest floor. This is your gift to the animal kingdom and it will magically complete the exchange of energy you have made with the environment.

Discover your Earth song

The Earth has many voices and sings a medley of songs if only we take the time to listen. Somewhere within the realm of the natural world will be a sound that moves you to your very core, a natural song that speaks to you on a magical level. I like to call such sounds Earth songs, and there are many out there to listen for. An Earth song might be the wind whispering in the leaves, long tall grasses sighing in a gentle breeze, the crash of ocean waves, the lapping of a pebble-filled stream, the chirping of grasshoppers or the dawn chorus. Discover which Earth song truly moves you (there may be more than one) and, if possible, spend time listening before spell-workings and meditations.

These days, of course, there is a vast number of 'sounds of nature' CDs available. Although it is preferable to attune with the real sound as nature plays it, sometimes this isn't possible, and a CD makes a useful substitute. These CDs also make available to us a whole range of sounds that nature generally keeps to herself, such as wolves howling, dolphins splashing, whales singing and Arctic icebergs colliding and melting into the sea. I have lots of nature sound CDs and I have found that they are a great way to enhance my magical castings, but I never get tired of listening to the sound of the leaves on the trees at the bottom of my garden rustling in the wind (the two large poplar trees are never still and remind me of gossipy old women).

If you are thinking of buying a nature sounds CD, take some time to think about which sounds mean the most to you. For me, for instance, the sound of the waves coming into shore is very evocative – it takes me straight back to my childhood. Try looking through your notes from the Earth Child Awareness exercise (see page 20) and see which Earth songs you were listening to. Or you could buy a collection of CDs and work your way through them, viewing this as a magical exercise and devoting yourself entirely to just listening.

Once you have discovered your personal Earth song, use it as a background to your spells, meditations and relaxation exercises. Earth songs are also a great way to help you fall asleep at night and can act as a gentle cure for mild insomnia.

Altars and shrines

Magic is a special process that deserves a special place of its own, and animal magic is no different. If you are pagan, or if you already practise magic in some way, you will probably already have an altar space set up. If so, you can either adapt this space for your animal magic or you can set up another space somewhere different. If you've never set up an altar before, don't worry. Below you will find some guidelines to help you go about it.

But first let's clarify the difference between an altar and a shrine, as many people wrongly assume that they are the same. They are not. An altar is a working area. It is here that you perform your spell-workings and keep your magical book. A shrine, on the other hand, is simply a place of worship. At a shrine you can meditate and make acknowledgement of who or what the shrine is dedicated to, you can light incense and candles as an act of reverence, but you do not work magic at a shrine. Sometimes the main function of a shrine is to prevent the altar from becoming overcrowded with statuettes and pictures. An altar is a work space and should never be cluttered.

If you do already have a working altar, a shrine can often be the most practical way of incorporating animal magic. You can then move a statue or picture of the creature you wish to work with to your main altar and work the spell there, afterwards returning the statue or picture to the shrine. This will enable you to work with more than one power animal without your altar becoming too full. If you have more than one power animal, you will need an individual shrine for each one.

Setting up an altar

To house your altar you will need a small table, the top of a chest of drawers or a similar space. Your altar is your working space and should be personal to you, but you should include the following:

- ✪ Two white candles in appropriate holders – called illuminator candles because they are used for illuminating the altar rather than for any symbolic purpose. They should be placed at the back of the altar.
- ✪ A pentacle – this is a five-pointed star surrounded by a circle. You can draw one on paper and cut it out if you do not have a proper Wiccan one. The pentacle should be placed in the centre of the altar.

Other objects that you might like to add to your altar include:

- ✪ An inscribing tool – a paper-knife will do fine if you don't have an athame (a witch's ritual knife).
- ✪ A wand – used by witches to direct power.
- ✪ A clear quartz crystal – this will keep the energy of your altar positive.
- ✪ Statues of the Lord of Animals and Lady of the Woods. For instance, I use as Lady of the Woods a lovely woodland sorceress figure who reminds me of Snow White. She wears a yellow dress and a dark green, hooded cloak. Trailing leaves and little white flowers are climbing over her, illustrating her connection with nature and the earth. On her arm she carries an owl, a creature symbolising wisdom and the Goddess, and the power of familiars in general.

Setting up a shrine

A shrine can be as simple as a collection of pictures hung on the wall or as elaborate as a range of statues with pictures, water features and so on. It's really up to you, your personal tastes, the space you have and the amount of cash you can afford to invest in your magic. Bear in

EARTH CHILD

mind, though, that animal magic is largely visionary. The trappings and tools are nice to have and fun to collect, but they are not essential. You can still make effective magic without them.

As we move through the book I will explain how to set up shrines to particular animals, making suggestions for possible decorations and variations on the traditional set-up. Meanwhile I suggest that you begin collecting pictures, postcards, statues and figures of any animals you think you might like to work with. These will be used later as a focus for your spell-castings.

Earth shadows

As part of your spell work you will need to create a magical Book of Earth Shadows. Earth shadows are all the spells and rituals you use in performing animals magic, and the Book of Earth Shadows is your record of them. If you are a practising witch, you may already have a Book of Shadows in progress and your Earth shadows could be included in this. Alternatively, you might want to create a special Book specifically for your animal magic.

If you are starting from scratch, you will need a blank note book. An A4 hardbound book, preferably in an earthy colour such as green or brown, works well. However, there is no right or wrong way to do this, so choose something that works for you. This is your book and will be unlike any other. Begin by copying the notes you made for the Earth Child Awareness exercise. Add any dreams, thoughts or reflections you have had about animals since beginning to read this book. Take your time to create your Earth Shadows Book – any magical book takes years to create and put together. It is an ongoing process, and the Book will grow as your magical abilities increase and develop.

Five-point Circle casting

Animal magic can be used anywhere, and the spells in this book are written in such as way as to be easy to memorise, thus giving you a wealth of familiars to call upon any time, any place, anywhere! However, some rituals benefit from the added strength of a magic

Circle. (If this is the case, it is clearly stated at the beginning of the spell.) Here is a simple Circle-casting technique for you to use in your workings of animal magic.

What you need
5 pillar candles in a neutral colour such as cream or white and appropriate candleholders (alternatively, you could use tea-lights), matches or a lighter

What you do

 Sit on the floor, facing your altar. Have the candles and the matches or lighter with you. Imagine that you are sitting in the centre of a clock face; your altar is at 12 o'clock.

 Place a candle on your altar, light it and say:

Akasha, spirit of all life.

 Place the second candle at 2 o'clock, light it and say:

Earth.

 Place a third candle at 4 o'clock, light it and say:

Air.

 Place a fourth candle at 8 o'clock, light it and say:

Fire.

 Finally, place the fifth candle at 10 o'clock, light it and say:

Water.

 Your Circle is now cast and you can begin your spell. To take down the Circle at the end of your ritual, simply snuff out the candles in reverse order, saying the name of the element followed by the words:

I release you.

So now you've set up your altar, enhanced your senses, attuned with nature and discovered your Earth song. You are now an Earth child, ready to take your first steps into the realm of magical beasts ...

Pet Therapy

The arrogance of science has conditioned us to believe in the concept of the food chain, with human beings at the top and all other creatures below us. Of course, it can't be denied that all animals need to eat other living things in order to survive, but the idea that there is some hierarchy involved seems to me absolutely wrongheaded. The notion of human superiority has no validity in metaphysical law, and I suggest that you push it to the back of your mind while you are working animal magic. Instead, I would like you to consider a concept that I call the circle of life. A circle has no top and no bottom; everything in the circle is therefore equal. If we consider ourselves as participating together with the animal kingdom and all living things in one vast circle, we begin to see a very different picture from the hierarchical food chain – a picture of equality.

If we expand this concept a little further and acknowledge that everything within the circle is connected, we begin to see the web of life. Of course, there are differences between life forms – for instance, some animals are carnivorous, others are herbivores – but, as inhabitants of the planet Earth, we each of us need all of this diversity, and through it we are all connected in some way.

Environmental scientists have proven again and again that in some instances animals can out-smart us, in spite of our vast wealth of technology! You may have seen instances of this animal wit on natural history TV programmes. And while you could try explaining to a hungry shark that you're at the top of the food chain and far out of his league, I dare say he wouldn't stop munching your limbs long enough to listen!

Does this mean that the shark is wicked? Do attacks on humans by sharks, tigers, wolves and so on, mean that these creatures are evil? Absolutely not. Take away our guns and technology and human beings have few natural defence mechanisms. This makes us a very easy target if we choose to invade the territory of large prey animals. If you go walking in the jungle, a tiger may well attack you because you're easy meat. This behaviour does not make the tiger evil; he is simply fulfilling his natural instincts and satisfying his need to eat. Incidentally, though, attacks on humans by wild animals are not as common as people seem to think. It is more usually we humans who kill our fellow creatures – sometimes in the name of sport. What does that say about us?

The feral pet

Deep inside every loving, loyal pet, lies the feral heart of a wild beast. This is most obvious if you share your home with cats and dogs, but clever observation of almost any animal will give you clues as to its natural instincts. For example, hibernating animals, such as hamsters, will store up little larders of food, despite living in centrally heated houses where they have no need to hibernate. Birds tend to fret and worry at their feathers if their cages are kept too low to the ground. As natural tree-dwellers, they feel vulnerable to attack. Place the cage high up and the bird will recover almost immediately.

Dogs will often scratch vigorously at their cosy blankets and fluffy beds, and will turn round and round in circles prior to settling down to sleep, curled up into a tight little ball. This behaviour stems from their ancestral relationship with wolves, who scratch and turn in long grass in order to flatten out a little bed in which they are hidden and safe – able to see, yet not be seen. They curl up in a ball to preserve their body heat in the cold. Cats do this too, often tucking their heads under their long tails and keeping just one eye in view. Of course, their ears are always pricked, listening out for signs of danger.

Domestic horses kept at grass in a field will turn and look directly at anything they are not sure of, ears pricked forward, their nostrils scenting the air, trying to detect danger. As prey animals, horses' main defence is flight, and even a tame pony will watch events and people closely, taking in every detail and gathering information. He will use this information to decide whether he needs to flee or if it is safe for him to continue grazing.

Whatever type of pet you have, observe it closely to discover its wild traits and natural instincts. This is the animal kingdom's reminder message, the way in which your pet says to you, 'You may think I belong to you, and I may be happy to live here, but I was wild once and could be wild again; I belong to no-one.' In fact, some animals, cats in particular, will take this sentiment one step further and add, 'It is you who belongs to me!' Anyone who has ever been 'owned' by a cat will understand the truth of this.

Pets as familiars

Those of you who regularly practise magic will know that spells can go wrong if you are feeling ill, depressed or just generally under the weather. The same thing can happen if a sick or unhappy animal is present in the Circle. If we want our pets to lend their energies to our magic as familiars, we must therefore practise responsible pet care.

In 99 cases out of 100 our pets did not choose to come and live with us. We went along to a pet shop, an animal breeder or a rescue centre, or answered a 'free to good home' ad. We picked the pet up and took it home with us. The pet in question had little or no choice in the matter. Of course, there are exceptions to this rule – such as the stray cat or dog who adopts us – but generally the pet we share our home with is there because we made the decision to have it. Therefore the least you can do in return is look after your pet responsibly. This means providing it with a warm, clean bed; a healthy diet made up of good, nutritious food; and fresh, clean water available at all times. These are the basics, the bare essentials, to which you will probably have to add some or all of the following: grooming, vaccinations, worming and pest control, veterinary check-ups and treatments, specialist care (such as shoeing a horse), toys, exercise, clipping and beauty treatments, tasty treats and, last but not least, your time and attention – and lots of it! A pet who is healthy, well tended, cared for and loved will be happy and secure – and prepared to return all your love and attention tenfold! It is this kind of pet that makes the best familiar.

Take a moment right now to make a list of anything your pet may need which you could have overlooked. Use the list above to help you. Then set about filling any deficiency.

Another way to make sure you are doing the best you can by your pet is to invest in one or two books written about its care and psychology. Or borrow books from the library. Read as much as you can about the history of the species and how its mind works. Learn about its body language so that you can read it at a glance and know instantly what it is trying to tell you. This is a way to begin to develop the deep communication that you will need to work magic together.

As communication develops between you and your pet, start to invite him into the magic Circle with you and ask that he lend his energies to your spell-castings. Remember that this is an invitation, and you should never force your pet to participate in a magic-working. Alternatively, you might like to work on a psychic connection with your pet.

Psychic links with pets

Animals, being creatures of instinct, have a natural psychic ability and can communicate easily with their human companions through mind power, or telepathy, as it is also called. Telepathy is the ability to project words and pictures into the mind of another, and to pick up these thought vibrations when they are sent to us. One of the main functions of a familiar is to pass information telepathically. It is up to you to be open to these links and to recognise a telepathic message when it comes.

Such information is not necessarily glamorous or even magical. Sometimes the message can be very simple. My cat, Pyewackett, is very good at sending such messages to me, usually late at night. I can be tucked up in bed, deeply absorbed in the book that I'm reading, and a picture will flash into my mind of Pye sitting on the wheelie bin, looking up at the bedroom window. Acting on this message, I go downstairs and open the back door. Sure enough, Pyewackett comes trotting into the house with a meow of thanks! Through his psychic abilities he is letting me know that he's finished his nocturnal rambles and would like to come in now please!

To develop such a link with your own pet, notice any images of him that come into your mind and then act upon them. It is very important that you do take action when you've had a message from your pet, as it will signal to him that the lines of communication are open and he will continue to send you messages, thus strengthening your psychic relationship over a period of time. You will then be able to use this link in your magic and spell-castings.

Another way that our pets can connect with us mentally is through empathy. This is the ability to feel someone else's emotions – a skill that animals make use of instinctively. Again, Pyewackett demonstrates this ability. Just recently my grandmother passed away and I was feeling sad. Pyewackett seemed to be equally distressed. He is a loyal cat and follows me around in any case, but during this troubled time he wouldn't leave my side for a second. He didn't go out for his daily rambles and was even off his food. He also became very vocal, often meowing loudly in my face as if to say, 'It's okay, I'm here!' His behaviour touched me deeply. Only after the funeral, when I showed signs of getting back on my feet, did Pye's behaviour return to normal.

Many of you will have similar stories of your own to tell, as empathy is one of the strongest and most easily recognisable forms of psychic link that our pets make with us. So if you're feeling down and your cat is insisting on attention or your dog is whining in your ear, don't push him aside with an irritable gesture, as this will only break any psychic connection your pet may have with you. Instead, pay attention and allow your pet's empathy to soothe your spirit as you gently stroke him. This will help to increase trust and affection between you, as well as strengthening the bond of witch and familiar.

The third type of psychic link with your pet can come through the medium of dreams. Should your pet appear in a dream, try to pay particular attention to how he looks, what he is doing and what is going on around him, as there could be a message for you hidden within these things. Keeping a dream diary will help you to discover this message and will enable you to see dream patterns, spot recurring dreams and so on.

To call a familiar

So you've read this far and you're fascinated by the concept of familiars. The problem is, at the moment you don't have a pet, and though you'd like to get one, you'd also like it to be natural familiar material. No problem! This spell will enable you to call the pet/familiar that is totally right for you. It was a spell similar to this one that brought Pyewackett to me, though I had to wait more than six months for him. Your familiar will come to you in his own time, and it is up to you to recognise him when he does, but first you have to summon him ...

What you need
A pen and a slip of paper

What you do
- ✪ On the slip of paper write down the kind of pet you want – cat, dog, rat, etc. Then think about colour, temperament, gender and any other characteristics and write these down too.
- ✪ Now build up a clear picture of your pet/familiar in your mind's eye. Talk to him, either out loud or in your head, and tell him that you will give him a safe and pleasant home, good food and lots of love and care – through sickness, health and old age. Also tell him that he will always remain free and you will never profess to own him. In return you'd like him to sit with you in the magical Circle and act as your familiar. Tell him that you will call him by the magical name of _____ (choose a suitable name).
- ✪ Now bury the slip of paper in the garden or in a potted plant. As you do this, and still holding the vision of your familiar in your mind, repeat these words three times:

> *I send these words on the spirit winds,*
> *A magical familiar here to bring.*
> *One of loyalty and temperament sweet,*
> *By powers of telepathy our minds will meet.*
> *Magical, affectionate, faithful and true,*
> *Powerful familiar I now call you.*
> *Come to me, by land, by sea;*
> *Come to me, I summon thee.*
> *Come to me, by earth, by air;*
> *Come to me my home to share.*
> *Come to me; do not hide.*
> *I summon thee to my side.*
> *So mote it be!*

PET THERAPY

Cat's Eyes

The best-known familiar of all is without a doubt the cat. As a creature of independence and mysterious habits, the cat will forever be associated with magic, and cats and witches are inextricably linked. Throughout history the cat has been both tortured and executed as a demon, and revered as a god, and cats still invoke strong responses in people today. The cat is a creature you either love or hate. Surrounded by folklore and superstition, it always maintains an air of mystery. Even those of us who have cats as pets never fully understand the lives of our feline companions. What exactly do they get up to when they leave the security of our homes? Where do they go? Just how far do they travel on their rambles? What does the night-time world look like through those beautiful jewel-like eyes?

During the Burning Times, when many women (and a few men) were executed for witchcraft, the cat fared just as badly. Many domestic cats were tortured and executed alongside the accused 'witches'. In one way, though, the cat had the last laugh, for with the feline population depleted, numbers of rats increased dramatically. With the rats came the fleas that carried the Black Death and later the Great Plague, both of which swept across Europe and the latter also across America. Too late, the cat's usefulness as a hunter was acknowledged, and slowly cats found their way back into domestic life.

But why were cats demonised in the first place? To answer this question we must look back to the various mythologies of the world. Many goddesses are associated with the cat. Diana and Artemis were said to have the ability to shape-shift into cats. Both goddesses are strongly linked to magic and witchcraft, and this could be where the idea of witches turning into cats came from. In Scotland the Cailleach Bheur, or Blue Hag of Winter, is associated with cats – the Highland wildcat in particular. The Roman goddess known in English as Liberty is often depicted with a cat at her feet, symbolising freedom and independence, while in Scandinavia the moon goddess Freya drove a chariot pulled by pure white cats. The Great Goddess of the Old Religion is also associated with the cat, through her sacred number, three. Three times three equals nine, the number of lives said to be allotted to the cat.

In ancient Egypt the status of the cat was so high that when a pet cat died, the household would shave off their eyebrows as a sign of mourning. Harming a cat in any way was punishable by death. Cats were often mummified and sent on their journey to the next life with elaborate funeral rites and grave gifts, and were generally buried in a cat cemetery. The Egyptians held cats sacred to Bast, whose name means 'soul of Isis'. Bast is the queen of all cats and is usually depicted with a woman's body and a feline head. She is a goddess of the Underworld, again linking cats with magic, witchcraft and darkness.

As the new religion of Christianity took hold throughout many parts of the world, the old beliefs were condemned as evil, and the sacred cat became a creature of the devil, regarded with fear and suspicion. In Europe and America, as I have said, many were executed during the Burning Times along with the witches. Cats were made into scapegoats and were banished from towns and villages. Many believed them to be miniature demons and would even refuse to speak in the presence of a cat lest it run off to tell its witch or the devil all that it had heard!

Fortunately, such dark and fearful times are long since past, and only a small grain of this illogical superstition survives today. And with the growing popularity of Wicca, paganism and other goddess- and earth-based religions, the cat is finally coming into its own again, sharing wisdom and working magic with those practitioners who will take the time to try to understand this mysterious creature.

Cat language

If you have a cat or are hoping to have one as your familiar, it is important to understand its psychology and body language so that you can build up a true connection. Until a few years ago I'd always considered myself to be a 'dog person'. When Pyewackett first came to live with me, I ignorantly believed that cats were just the same as lap dogs but with smaller ears, longer tails and sharper claws! However, Pyewackett has taught me better, and I now know that cats are like no other creature on Earth. Here are a few hints on the subtle art of understanding cat language.

In general, purring is a sign of happiness and contentment, but it can also be an indication of pain or fear, so listen carefully to the tone of the purr and keep your eyes open for any signs of illness or injury. As we stroke our cats we are unconsciously imitating the action of a mother cat licking her kittens. As a result, the cat will often respond with kitten behaviour, such as kneading with his front paws, as he used to knead his mother's stomach to stimulate the milk flow.

A nose-to-nose greeting from your cat is a sign that he trusts you completely. It is also a way for him to detect where you have been since he was last in contact with you. Another sign of trust is turning on his back and allowing you to tickle his tummy. Pyewackett loves this kind of attention, but some cats hate it and will bite or scratch, so be wary! The movement of a cat's tail is a good way of detecting his mood. Gentle swaying or flicking the end of the tail indicates a happy, sociable cat. However, if the whole of the tail flicks rapidly from side to side, your cat is not happy and may wish to be left alone! Holding the tail up stiffly in the air and fluffing it out is a sign of aggression and sometimes fear, while a tail tucked out of sight as the cat crouches to the floor and flattens his ears is an unequivocal sign of fear.

As solitary hunters, cats are very territorial and will fight quite viciously to protect their patch. Leaving scent messages is a way of marking out the boundaries and staking a claim to areas, objects or even people. With scent glands at various points on their body, including the top of their head, cats will rub against people and objects around them to leave their scent and make their property known. They also spray urine as a way of marking their territory. As well as to check out who's been on their patch, female cats sniff a tom cat's spray to detect whether or not he is a suitable mate. You could say this is the feline equivalent to a blind date!

If a cat is unsure of something or someone, his instinct is to get up high. Trees, walls, fences and so on are useful for this; indoors, staircases and cupboard tops provide excellent vantage points from which to survey the scene around. Cats also seem to think that if they can't see you, you can't see them and will close their eyes as a sign of dismissal! Perhaps the most effective way to communicate with your cat is through eye contact. Never stare at a cat. Catch his eye, blink once and then look away. This is a non-threatening communication and will invite friendship and trust. If your cat is staring at you, simply blink at him and then hold his gaze for a few moments. In all likelihood he will blink back and then settle down, knowing that all is well.

Cats have a thoroughly independent spirit and their lust for freedom is legendary. However, if we take the time to build up a relationship with them, they will demonstrate incredible loyalty to us in return. In the feline mind, though, it is we who belong to them. In other words, I am Pyewackett's human; he is not my cat! This is a wonderful twist to the way people generally regard their pets – and only a cat could turn such thinking on its head and demonstrate his point so forcefully! A cat will only be fussed if it suits him. However, if you are busy or in the middle of something important he will choose that moment to demand your complete attention! Personally, I believe that cats have never forgotten their former elevated status and insist on reminding us of their superiority as often as they can!

Colour magic

In magical terms the colour of your feline familiar can indicate the type of magic he is best suited to assist you with. Traditionally, black cats are by far the luckiest and are a good all-rounder when it comes to spell-castings and witchcraft. All cats are said to bring some form of luck, however, and the colour of their coat may illustrate the kind you can expect.

Ginger cats bring financial luck and should be called into your Circle when you perform money and abundance spells, or any magic that concerns your business or career. Tortoiseshell cats bring luck in love and affairs of the heart, while a black and white cat is lucky for children and family matters, so a great pet for a small child or newly weds. A tabby cat will bring protection and luck to your home, a grey cat will bring you much wisdom and prophetic dreams, and a multi-coloured cat will ensure that you are never without friends. Finally, a pure white cat can assist you with matters of creativity, inspiration, fortune-telling and divination. White cats are also said to be the earthly representatives of the Celtic Faerie Cat, or Spirit Cat. This elemental being shows itself to you just prior to great change in your life. Whether the change be good or bad, only time will tell, but the Spirit Cat comes to warn you that it is imminent.

Choose your feline wisely, unless he has already chosen you. But don't be so wed on having, say, a ginger familiar that if a tabby one makes itself known to you, you don't notice.

Cats as barometers

Careful observation of your cat can give an indication as to what kind of weather to expect over the following 24 hours. A cat who sits close by the fire is generally warning of frost and snow, while one who sleeps all day is thought to be preparing for a clear, starry night ahead. If your cat finds himself a quiet nook, a storm is approaching; and if he is suddenly skittish and won't settle, it is a sign of strong winds and gales to come. A cat who washes only his face and ears is foretelling rainfall, while one who stretches out contentedly is indicating a spell of good weather ahead.

Cats as old souls

In some belief systems, the final incarnation of a soul comes to Earth as a cat. This is the soul's holiday time, when it has learnt all it needs to learn and comes back just to party, before moving on to a higher plane of existence. It is thought that the reason cats have nine lives (in the adage anyway) is so that the soul has the chance to make the most of its final visit to Earth. And let's face it, for the most part the life of a cat is pretty good – all they seem to do is eat, drink, sleep, mate and spend every night out on the tiles! Not to mention ruling the household in which they live – can't be bad!

Creating a cat shrine

To make the most of your cat's magical energies or to use the cat as your familiar even if you don't have one as a pet, it helps to set up a small shrine to your feline friends. First, find a small surface – a shelf will do – and give it a good clean. Create your shrine by placing upon it pictures and statuettes of cats, as well as items of general feline relevance. For example, you could put a photograph of your cat in the centre, together with a small pot of catnip (cats adore this plant). An oil burner with a feline theme would be appropriate, as would figures of Egyptian-style cats. A figure of Bast would make the shrine a truly sacred space.

Remember also to acknowledge the wildness of the cat in some way. You could do this very simply by including a postcard of a lion or, more elaborately, by hanging a tiger tapestry on the wall above. If wildcats are your thing, then your shrine could be totally made up of tigers, lions, panthers, leopards and so on. However, you might still like to honour Bast in some way – perhaps with a picture or statue – as she is the queen of all cats, both wild and domestic.

It is at this shrine that you will connect with any thought-form cats that you have conjured and will ask for your pet cat to be protected. Keep the shrine clean and tidy, and try to burn a little catnip incense here regularly in order to deepen the connection between yourself and your familiar.

A naming spell

If you wish to have a real cat as your familiar, you will need to give him a magical name. You may want to make up your own name for your cat, or you might like to choose a traditional name. There are many of these, including, for male cats, Pyewackett, Hecuba, Merlin, Ambrose,

Llewellyn, Marmaduke, Nicodemus and Nostradamus and, for female cats, Esmerelda, Angelica, Petronella, Griselda, Gerta, Freya, Hecate, Morrigan and Isis. Once you have your name, you are ready to perform this naming spell.

What you need

Matches or a lighter, a figure of Bast (optional), your cat, your cat's comb or brush, a slip of paper and a pen, your cauldron or a heat-proof bowl

What you do

✪ Take your cat with you to your altar room and light the illuminator candles upon the altar. If you are using a figure of Bast, place this upon the altar too.

✪ Sit before your altar with your cat on your knee, softly stroking him and talking to him gently. Tell him that you practise magic and would like him to help you as your familiar. In return, promise the cat your love, care and attention for as long as he lives.

✪ Gently begin to groom your cat. Collect a little of his fur from the comb or brush. Write your cat's magical name on the slip of paper and fold the fur within it, saying:

> I name this cat ———. He is now my magical familiar and we are bound together by the power of the Craft. So mote it be!

✪ Use one of the illuminator candles to light the spell paper and allow it to burn in your cauldron or the heat-proof bowl.

Invoking a panther of protection

If you ever need a little extra protection, then call on the wild black panther for assistance. As the largest of lucky black cats, the panther can assist you by acting as a bodyguard on lonely night-time walks, or by patrolling your property through the darkest hours. This is a visionary spell wherein you will conjure up a thought form and direct its power to where you feel you need it most. You can enhance the magic by giving the thought form a name and by placing a picture or statue of a panther on your cat shrine. Reading up about panthers before you perform the spell will also increase its potency.

This spell can also be adapted to create a thought form of any other creature you wish to work with.

What you need
5 pillar candles in white or a neutral colour, matches or a lighter, a picture of a panther (optional)

What you do
- ✪ Go to your altar and cast a circle using the five pillar candles as described on page 29.
- ✪ If you are using a picture, focus on the image of the panther. Otherwise, close your eyes and bring to your mind the image of a very large black panther – we're talking Beast of Bodmin Moor here, so think big!
- ✪ With your finger, draw the outline of the panther in the air before you, making sure he is life-sized.
- ✪ Slowly and steadily breathe life into him by blowing gently into the outline, filling it with the magical breath of life. Do this three times.
- ✪ In your mind's eye, visualise the panther looking at you intently, waiting for your instructions. Tell the panther what you want him to do (protect you, your house, your car – the choice is yours).
- ✪ Watch as the panther bounds off to do your bidding, or remains close to you if you've asked him to protect you.
- ✪ You have now created a thought form and have brought a powerful familiar into your life. Remember to instruct the familiar daily and to set him free when his job is complete. To do this, return to your altar, call your panther to mind and say:

> *I give you thanks for protecting me so well. Go now. I release you. Come again when I have need of you. Blessed be!*

To protect your cat

For this spell you will need a charm or talisman to attach to your cat's collar. A pentacle is ideal, but feel free to choose any that feels suitable to you. Be aware that cats who roam often lose their collars, so don't pick anything too pricey. If this does happen, you will need to repeat the spell with a new charm and collar.

What you need
5 pillar candles in white or a neutral colour, matches or a lighter, your pentacle, a disk or charm to put on your cat's collar, your cat's collar

What you do
⭐ Go to your altar and use the pillar candles to cast a circle, as described on page 29.

⭐ Place your chosen charm in the centre of the five-pointed star on your pentacle. Hold your hands over it, palms down, and envision a strong white light moving from your hands down into the charm. This process is known as charging, and it empowers an object for magical use. As you continue to charge the charm, say:

> *I call on Bast, queen of cats. I ask that she offer extra protection to my feline familiar,* —— (state the magical name of your cat). *I empower this magical talisman with the power of protection against all harm, and as a sign that my cat is now charmed. So mote it be!*

⭐ Attach the charm to your cat's collar and put it on your cat.

Quick protection charm

I use this simple protection chant whenever I let Pyewackett out for his rambles. If the Goddess is not part of your religious beliefs, you can call upon any other spiritual power that has significance for you.

What you do

⭐ Using the magical name of your own cat, say (out loud or in your head:

> *Goddess, protect —— from all harm around;*
> *Goddess, protect —— and keep him safe and sound.*

To prevent your cat from straying

What you need
A little fur from your cat's comb or brush, an envelope, a slip of paper with your full address written on it, a small leaf from your garden or a houseplant, your pentacle

What you do

⭐ Go to your altar and pluck out three hairs from your own head. If possible, twist them around the cat fur.

⭐ Place the hair and the fur in the envelope, together with the slip of paper and the leaf. These items will magically link together yourself, your cat, your home and your garden.

⭐ Seal the envelope and write your cat's name on the front, followed by the words 'do not stray'.

⭐ Place the envelope on the pentacle on your altar for three days, then put it somewhere safe where it won't be lost or accidentally discarded. You could tape it into your book of shadows or keep it together with any magical tools you own. Alternatively, place it in the bottom of your underwear drawer or somewhere else that only you have access to – but it must be kept within the house.

Cat return spell

If your cat has been missing for 24 hours or more and all else has failed, try this spell to bring him back safely. It has always brought my own cat safely home within the hour. This spell first appeared in my book *Everyday Spells for a Teenage Witch*.

What you need
A few cat treats, your (clean) cat's bowl

What you do

⭐ Place the cat treats in the bowl and visualise your cat safe at home with you. As you do this, repeat the following charm nine times, one for each feline life:

> *Bring the cat I love and feed;*
> *Bring him home with all due speed.*
> *I accept that he will roam;*
> *Protect him on his journey home.*
> *A true companion I have found,*
> *So let my cat be homeward bound.*
> *Before the passing of one more day*
> *Let my cat come home to stay.*
> *Bring him to me safe at last.*
> *This I ask of you, Queen Bast.*
> *So mote it be!*

Good luck spell

Black cats are considered to be very lucky by witches and magical people, so if you would like to bring a run of good luck into your life or put an end to any bad luck you feel you may have been having, call on the powers of the black cat. The Good Luck Spell should be performed on the night of the full moon.

This spell calls for a black candle shaped like a cat. These are available from most occult stores and some new age outlets, but if you have difficulty obtaining one, then buy a plain black candle instead and carve the word 'cat' into the wax, using your inscribing tool.

What you need
5 pillar candles in white or a neutral shade, matches or a lighter, a black candle shaped like a cat or with the word 'cat' inscribed in it, a suitable candleholder

What you do
⭐ Place the cat candle in the holder and put it at the centre of your altar.

⭐ Light the cat candle, concentrate on the flame and chant the following, continuing as long as you remain focused:

> *Black cat, black cat, I ask of you this boon:*
> *Fill my life with happiness and bring me good luck soon.*
> *Black cat, black cat, I ask of you this boon:*
> *Bring lots of luck into my life, beginning this full moon.*

⭐ Blow out the candle. Keep it in a safe place ready to use for future good luck spells.

Talisman of feline energy

A great way to keep cat energy and feline protection with you all day long is to carry a tiger's eye crystal. These crystals are brown and amber in colour, and usually have a striped appearance, hence the name! Such crystals are widely available and usually cost about £1 for a small polished tumble stone.

What you need
A small tiger's eye crystal

What you do
⭐ Place the tiger's eye crystal on your pentacle to charge for nine days. Then pop it in your wallet or purse and keep it with you at all times, drawing on the strength of the cat species.

To increase your independence

Cats, both wild and domestic, are famed for their independent streak. If you would like more independence in your own life, then call on the energies of the cat by performing this simple rite.

What you need
An image of a cat (this could be a photo of your pet, or a statue or picture of a wildcat), a tea-light and a suitable holder, matches or a lighter

What you do
- Sit before your altar and focus your attention on the image of the cat.
- Light the tea-light, place it in the holder and say these words (or others of your own creation):

  Sacred spirit of the cat, I honour you. I admire your independence, your assertiveness and your freedom of spirit. I ask that you teach me your ways that I may live my life blessed with your gifts and achieve a freedom and independence of spirit that truly uplifts and empowers me. I welcome your gifts and your teachings into my life. Blessed be!

- Decide on three small acts of independence to perform on the next three days. Write them down and promise yourself that you will do them. (If you do this, you will soon begin to experience the independence that you crave.)
- While the tea-light burns down, spend a little time doing something 'catty' – watching a wildlife programme about big cats, interacting with your pet cat or reading up on feline psychology.

Lion strength

To increase your sense of inner strength, attune with the lion, king of cats and true survivor! How you attune depends on you and your lifestyle. You could adopt the lion as your power animal and build a shrine to him in your house. You could hang pictures of lions on your wall, visit the zoo, watch documentaries about lions or read about them. Then, whenever you are facing a challenge in life, consider yourself a lion and you will be able to draw on the strength of this courageous familiar.

(Of course, this spell, could be adapted to suit any of the big cats, so if tigers are more your thing, focus on them instead.)

The Beast of Bodmin Moor

In recent years there have been a number of sightings of big, black, wild cats, the most famous being the Beast of Bodmin Moor. Large black cats are reputedly now wandering around the British countryside, and a new collection of urban myths has arisen surrounding them. When the skull of a large cat was found on Bodmin Moor, the nation waited with baited breath – only to be told by scientists that research had proven the skull to belong to a leopard-skin rug. But surely leopard-skin rugs were once leopards? And panthers are after all a member of the leopard species ... The mystery remains unsolved.

Wolf Cult

Some familiars have a darker history than others. Wolves and other members of the canine species hold a sometimes sinister place within our folklore and story-telling history, with whisht hounds, killer wolves, Black Shuck, werewolves and even spectral foxes bounding through the pages of traditional British mythology. At the same time, dogs are often represented as paragons of loyalty. The faithful domestic dog does its utmost to protect us, often resulting in a dog-eat-dog scenario. Legend gives us two sides to the canine coin: the wild wolf and the faithful hound.

The canine species has none of the subtlety and stealthiness of the feline. When wolf energy is around, you will know about it! When your dog wants his walk, he will communicate his request until he gets what he wants. Canines do not have the ability seemingly to appear and disappear at will as cats do, but they do have a strength and a stamina that enables them to be powerful protectors and great burglar alarms! Nor do they crave freedom and independence. A dog will give himself over to you completely and will work and live and die for you if needs be. Perhaps the happiest homes, then, are those that house both dogs and cats, containing an all-round spectrum of familiar energy.

For centuries dogs have worked closely with humankind – as hunters and retrievers, as protectors and guardians of homes and property, and as herders and watchers of farm animals. In modern times the role of the dog has expanded to include sniffing out drugs and explosives, maintaining law and order as canine officers within the police force, and generally cheering up the sick and elderly as therapy visitors to hospitals and homes. Dogs are the eyes of the blind, the ears of the deaf and the general helpers of the disabled. They are also our much beloved pets and companions. But they haven't always been man's best friend ...

Cry wolf

At one time the length and breadth of Britain was densely populated by wolves. The full moon of January is traditionally called the Wolf Moon, as it was during this time that hungry wolves would come in from the wilderness, raiding towns and villages in search of food. In January, too, wolf-hunting was a traditional pastime. Many wolves were slaughtered and their pelts were used to bring a degree of warmth to draughty castles and manor houses, being fashioned into floor rugs and bed covers, warm cloaks and capes, mittens and muffs. Wolves were greatly feared and were considered to be creatures of the devil and indiscriminate killers.

As you will see throughout this book, any animal that was once held sacred to the Goddess and the Old Ways, later became demonised with the rise of Christianity. It was in this troubled time of spiritual conflict that many legends and superstitions grew up around particular animals – especially those associated with paganism, goddess worship and witchcraft.

The wolf is one of these creatures, and he has suffered greatly as a result of misinformation and suspicion. In paganism the wolf is sacred to Mars, the Roman god of war, and also to the Morrigan, the Celtic goddess of war. The Celts used semi-tame wolves to good effect during battle, and wolves became known as the 'dogs of war'. Wolves are also associated with Merlin, the most powerful wizard of all, who kept a wolf as his familiar, thus linking this animal to magic and witchcraft. Their domestic cousin, the dog, is sacred to Hecate, protective goddess of witches and queen of the Underworld. In some traditions it is a dog who guards the entrance to the Underworld, for instance the Egyptian Anubis or the Greek three-headed Cerberus. And who can forget Fluffy from the Harry Potter books?!

As Christianity evolved, the Old Ways were suppressed and wolves came to be regarded as evil and a very real threat. They were hunted almost to the point of extinction and were regarded with such contempt that during the Middle Ages an outlaw would be known as a 'wolfshead'. How fitting it is that the most famous 'wolfshead' of all is, of course, Robin Hood, an aspect of the witch's god and a symbol of paganism. Even in such dangerous times the Old Religion just refused to disappear.

Wolves are now a protected species. Their numbers are being carefully monitored and they are being reintroduced into parts of Scotland, America and Canada. Hopefully, future generations of the human race will be a great deal kinder and more understanding towards these beautiful and highly intelligent creatures, and will help them to thrive in the wild unhindered. Our fears of and superstitions about the wolf have thankfully subsided and have been replaced with sound scientific knowledge of these creatures and their habits. But the legends survive ...

Werewolves

Lycanthropy is the more scientific term for the werewolf phenomenon. A person bitten by a wolf reputedly takes on aspects of the wolf's character, turning into a wolf themselves at the time of the full moon. Werewolf stories are found throughout Europe and have turned a pretty penny for the movie makers! In the Balkans it is believed that upon his death a werewolf becomes a vampire, and these two characters are frequently linked together, proving the truth of the adage that there is no rest for the wicked!

Magically speaking, the werewolf provides a metaphor for the good and bad to be found in mankind; it symbolises the light and the dark, and the inner struggle to synthesise them harmoniously. The werewolf is a supernatural predator, who clearly illustrates that giving in entirely to the dark side can only result in eventual self-destruction. His association with the full moon may well be one root of our modern term 'lunacy' – the madness of the moon. It also links him, as a demonic aspect of the once-sacred wolf, back to the Goddess. Interestingly, a werewolf can only be killed with a silver bullet. As silver is the metal of the Goddess, perhaps this is an indication that a werewolf can only be absolved and given peace by returning to her. Perhaps in her arms he can become wolf once again – a creature to be honoured and revered, not reviled and feared.

The whisht hounds

All over Britain tales of phantom black dogs – or whisht hounds – abound. Up and down the country you will find Black Dog Inns and Black Dog Lanes, all referring to the ancient belief in 'old padfoot'. Some whisht hounds haunt in packs; others are solitary apparitions, such as the one immortalised in Sir Arthur Conan Doyle's book *The Hound of the Baskervilles*. Generally, they are harbingers of impending disaster or doom.

According to most legends, such creatures are reasonably friendly and come only to serve as a warning that you should alter your present course if you wish to avoid disaster. In some legends, however, the black dog haunts a specific area, usually a dirt track or stretch of road, that was once the scene of violence. In Newton St Cyres, for instance, the black dog paces the spot where a young girl was brutally murdered. Criminologists believe that the temptation to return to the scene of the crime is too great for most criminals to resist; some folklorists hold that the black dogs are waiting for this return in order to claim the criminal's darkened soul.

In Norfolk old padfoot is known as Black Shuck, from the Anglo Saxon word *scucca*, meaning 'demon'. To some, Black Shuck is a devil dog indeed and is reputed to have eyes that weep red fire. He is often regarded with fear by the local people, but to those of a magical turn of mind he can be called upon to prevent someone doing you harm. A witch can send Black Shuck to an enemy to 'see him off' – with the proviso that he do harm to none, a traditional rider to all ethical witches' spells.

Large black dogs are said to carry the essence of Black Shuck or old padfoot, so if you have one as a pet, you can enhance your relationship with him by studying the old legends. You could also buy an A–Z of your local area and look out for any Black Dog Lanes and such like. Visit these areas and see what your intuition can pick up. Visit first in daylight and again in the darkness of the night, taking a like-minded friend with you for safety. If you have a dog, make a third visit and carefully observe his reaction to the area to see what he picks up. Write your findings in your Earth Shadows book under an appropriate heading – such as Old Padfoot or Whisht Hounds.

Brave Gerlert

I can clearly remember, as a small child in school, sitting in assembly and hearing our headmaster, who was a proud Welshman, tell us the story of Gerlert. The following summer, on a family holiday in Wales, I also remember standing in front of Gerlert's grave and recounting the tale to my family.

The wonderful tale of Gerlert is one that I will carry with me all my life – for its tragedy, for its message of unmistakable courage and true loyalty, and for its reflection of the way in which humankind often repays its canine friends. This is a true story that has passed into legend and been handed down through the generations. It clearly illustrates the shadow and light of the canine world and the dog's fragile relationship with human beings. It therefore has a place within this book, and I will tell the tale briefly in my own words.

Long ago, in the thirteenth century, there lived a Welsh hero known as Prince Llywellyn the Great. One morning, Prince Llywellyn decided to go out hunting, so he saddled his horse and rode off into the forest, leaving his trusty hound Gerlert to guard his little baby son, who was fast asleep in the crib.

Now the winter had been hard and spring seemed a long way off, and the wolves who lived in the wild were forced to come close to the villages in search of food. It was one of these wolves who happened to find his way into Llywellyn's house, where an infant lay unprotected ... or so the wolf thought. For, as he saw the wolf, the faithful Gerlert sprang from the shadows to defend his master's child from the intruder.

The wolf and the hound fought tooth and claw, and in the fray the crib was overturned and the baby began to cry with fright. The wolf was large and strong, and hunger made him vicious, but Gerlert was a match for him and, though sorely injured, he eventually managed to overcome the wolf and kill it. Gerlert then limped across the room and lay down to lick his wounds by the fallen crib, ready to protect his master's child should other wolves appear.

And so it was that when Prince Llywellyn returned home he found his baby's crib overturned and his hound covered in blood, licking his lips. Grief and rage consumed Llywellyn, and in an instant he had drawn his mighty sword and plunged it to the hilt through poor Gerlert's faithful breast. Then, wiping the tears from his eyes, he went to the crib to say his final goodbyes to the child who would never grow to be a man. And what did he find but the carcass of a great, bloody wolf, his teeth still bared in death, and his own tiny son kicking and gurgling in the safety of the upturned crib.

Only then did the stark reality of the situation come upon poor Llywellyn and, realising what he had done, he cried: 'Oh, brave Gerlert! Your faithful courage and stout heart shall never be forgotten!'

Gathering the large hound in his strong arms, Llywellyn went outside to dig poor Gerlert's grave. There he laid Gerlert, the most loyal dog that ever lived. Over the grave he erected a magnificent tombstone inscribed with the story of brave Gerlert. It is said that Prince Llywellyn never had another hound.

So ends the sad story of Gerlert. If you are ever in Wales and get the chance to visit Gerlert's grave, do pay your respects to this faithful dog who was ill rewarded for his loyalty by his master. And try to remember, too, that our dogs only ever want to please us and they live for our approval. It is up to us to be as faithful to them as they are to us.

WOLF CULT

The wolf in our homes

Careful observation of our pet dogs can give us a glimpse of their wild side and wolfish nature. By understanding canine mentality we can develop a close relationship with them and can nurture a pack-like environment rather than the master–slave scenario that unfortunately many dogs have to endure.

Dogs, like wolves, are pack animals, and in the wild they will remain within their family unit within the pack throughout their lives. Within the pack each animal has its own place and knows its role. There is a strict hierarchy and feeding routine.

To our dogs we are the pack, and their place within that pack is determined by our behaviour towards them. Much of the dog's wild role has been taken from him. For instance, wolves procreate to ensure the survival of the species and also their own pack line. Domestic dogs are often neutered or spayed, or else they are allowed to breed only according to a breeder's programme. Wolves also hunt for their food, their success depending on co-operation and team work. Domestic dogs are handed a bowl of food to a schedule that suits their human companions.

The key, then, to a healthy, fulfilling relationship with your dog is to understand pack life. First of all, it is important that your dog sees you as the alpha within the pack, the top dog. Only then will you have an obedient, well-behaved animal who can be taken anywhere. You should never hit your dog as a punishment. Dogs don't understand violent punishments but they will rise up and defend themselves against abuse. By hitting your dog you are effectively training him to be vicious. It is far better to banish your dog temporarily from the pack, by sending him into another room for a short while. Dogs fear banishment, since in the wild a wolf who has been banished is almost certain to die of starvation or to be killed by another pack. When your dog rejoins the family, continue to ignore him for a while – this is the way canine females deal with unruly pups. By adopting such training methods you are teaching your dog how you want him to behave using methods he already understands and accepts at an innate level. By the way, it is a fallacy that you cannot teach an old dog new tricks – it will certainly take longer and you will need much patience, but it can be done.

Read as much as you can about dogs, wolf packs and pack training methods, then apply what you learn to your own dog. To get you started, here are a few wolfish behaviours to look out for in your dog. Rolling over on to their back is a sign of submission in dogs and an indication that they view you as a higher member of the pack. By the same token, dogs who are snappish with children view them as lower pack members – puppies who need to be put in their place by older dogs.

Begging for food from the table is another indication that your dog sees you as a higher pack member, and he will wait patiently, his eyes fixed on you, until he discovers whether or not you have left him any scraps. This is classic pack behaviour and stems from the strict feeding hierarchy that wolves have.

When a dog licks your face it is harking back to puppy behaviour, as wolf pups will lick the muzzle of a parent or older wolf to persuade them to regurgitate food. This also explains why domestic dogs have been known to eat vomit! To the dog, however, this is just another natural pack behaviour.

But not all canine habits are – to the human mind – quite so yucky! Dogs make excellent guard animals because they are used to defending their territory and protecting the pack. They also make excellent jogging companions because wolves can cover vast areas of territory quite quickly and are renowned for their stamina. And a faithful dog will protect your children, as within the pack wolf aunts can act as nannies and babysitters.

But here is where the true magic lies ... in sharing your life with a dog, you have in effect, invited the wolf into your home and become a trusted and valued member of his pack! It is up to you to do everything you can to be worthy of such trust and never to betray it. Once you have the love and loyalty of your dog, betrayal can only come from one source: you. Your dog will live only to please you and will protect you and your family valiantly.

Creating a wolf shrine

Images of wolves are very popular at the moment, and there has probably never been a better time to set up a wolf shrine, as the shops are full of them. If you feel that you will be working wolf magic quite regularly, you might like to set up a full working altar dedicated to the wolf and canine species in general. Alternatively, you might prefer a smaller and simpler shrine. Choose a shrine that fits the amount of space you have available and the amount of money you can spend on it. The following tips will work as well for a very basic shrine as for an elaborate working set-up.

My own wolf shrine is located in the hallway and staircase of my house. It consists of a series of pictures of wolves in snowy settings (winter is my favourite season) along with wrought-iron candle sconces hung between the frames. A picture of a beautiful black wolf with gleaming amber eyes hangs opposite my front door, and he glares at anyone who dares to invade my privacy! I plan to add to this shrine over time, placing statues on windowsills and small tables – creating a beautiful shrine or altar is always an ongoing process.

You could create a similar shrine to mine on a wall in your house, or you could go for a more traditional table shrine, including, for example, statues of wolves (there are some wonderful Native American ones available), a wolf-style water feature and maybe even a couple of foxes. Add a candle or two, a little incense and a photograph of your dog, and place a couple of faux wolf-fur cushions on the floor before the shrine and you are all set up and ready to go. To turn this space into an altar, add any tools that you have, such as a pentacle, an athame (or ritual knife), a cauldron or a wand. If you have opted for a working wolf altar, make sure your chosen surface has ample working space.

To call the wolves

In witchcraft, we often call in spirits or elementals at each compass point of the Circle in order to enhance the power of our magic. These compass points are called 'the quarters' and inviting in the elementals is known as 'calling the quarters'. The following quarter calls can be used to invoke wolf energy at the four quarters of your magic Circle.

What you need
5 pillar candles in white or a neutral colour, matches or a lighter

What you do

- Using the pillar candles, cast the circle, following the instructions given on page 29.
- Standing inside the circle, face north, raise your arms high above your head in invocation and speak the following incantation:

> *I call the Snowy Wolf from the Arctic Northlands.*
> *Guard my space with tooth and claw.*
> *I bid you welcome. Blessed be!*

- Now face east, raise your arms high above your head in invocation and speak the following incantation:

> *I call the Silver Wolf from the Dawn Realms.*
> *Guard my space with tooth and claw.*
> *I bid you welcome. Blessed be!*

- Now face south, raise your arms high above your head in invocation and speak the following incantation:

> *I call the Golden Wolf from the Desert Sands.*
> *Guard my space with tooth and claw.*
> *I bid you welcome. Blessed be!*

- Now face west, raise your arms high above your head in invocation and speak the following incantation:

> *I call the Midnight Wolf of the Shadow Lands.*

Guard my space with tooth and claw.
I bid you welcome. Blessed be!

⚙ When you have finished working your magic and are ready to close the Circle, go around it in the opposite direction, beginning in the west, and say to each of the wolf energies you have called:

Great Wolf, I give you thanks for your protection, and I release
you. Go with my love. Blessed be!

To gather information

This visualisation exercise requires nothing but your imagination.

What you do

⚙ Shortly before going to sleep at night, close your eyes and call to mind the spirit of a wolf or the familiar spirit of your own dog. Visualise this astral spirit clearly and try to make contact with him.

⚙ Once you have his full attention, address him with the following words:

Sacred spirit of the wolf, I have summoned you here because I
have need of your skills. I request that you work on my behalf
gathering all the information you can regarding —— (state
your purpose). *Use your keen ears, use your sharp eyes, travel*
far and wide if you must, but remember always your purpose.
Bring the information I require. Come to me in the shadow
lands and tell me all I wish to know. Go now and do my
bidding. Blessed be!

⚙ Visualise the wolf bounding off to carry out your orders, and make a note of your dreams during the following nights, as the information you seek will be brought to you in sleep by your wolf familiar.

To overcome enemies

If someone is giving you a hard time, threatening you or treating you badly in any way, send a wolf to see them off. This spell harms none but will give your enemies enough of a fright to make them think twice before targeting you again. It works wonderfully on nasty neighbours!

What you need
5 pillar candles in white or a neutral colour, matches or a lighter, a picture of a wolf (optional), a slip of paper, a black pen, your pentacle

What you do
- Using the pillar candles, cast the circle, following the instructions on page 29.
- Using the picture of a wolf if you choose, or just closing your eyes and using your imagination, call to mind a huge wolf, whatever colour you like, and visualise him clearly. I usually work with either a black wolf or a blue-grey one.
- Using the black pen, write down the name of your enemy on the slip of paper and place it on your pentacle to charge.
- Remaining focused on your chosen wolf, repeat the following charm three times:

  > *Who's afraid of the big, bad wolf?*
  > *Who screams and runs in fright?*
  > *Who's afraid of the big, bad wolf*
  > *That stalks my foe this night?*
  > *I am no victim of attack,*
  > *So this is now my game.*
  > *I send a wolf out from my pack*
  > *Who will my enemy tame!*
  > *So mote it be!*

- Visualise the wolf going off to carry out your command.
- Burn the slip of paper bearing your enemy's name. The spell is complete and your foe should leave you alone, but if not, repeat the spell on the night of the full moon for added power.

For battle strength

The purpose of this spell is not to send you off to war, but to give you a wolf-like strength when facing the battles of life. This spell calls on the god Mars and the goddess Morrigan, so if you have statues or pictures of these deities, place them on your altar before you start working.

What you need
5 pillar candles in white or a neutral shade, matches or a lighter, a tea-light and a suitable holder

What you do
⭐ Use the pillar candles to cast a circle, following the instructions on page 29.

⭐ Call to mind the image of a wolf and focus on it strongly. Then spend a little time contemplating the particular struggle or challenge you are facing right now.

⭐ When you are ready, light the tea-light and speak the following charm:

> *Mars and Morrigan, bring your wolves;*
> *Bring on the dogs of war.*
> *I face a battle in my life;*
> *Defeat I'll know no more.*
> *Lend me canine courage and strength,*
> *Reveal my path to me,*
> *Give me valour that I at length*
> *Shall taste of victory!*

⭐ Allow the tea-light to burn down completely. You should feel a renewed strength and a sense of positivity within the next 24 hours, and you should be able to overcome all the challenges you faced at the time of casting the spell.

To help you through the dark days

This spell first appeared in my book *The Witch's Almanac 2004*, but it has a place within these pages as it calls on the strength of the wolf for protection. The beauty of this spell is that if you learn the charm by heart, you can cast it anywhere, at any time, whenever you need protection or additional strength.

What you do

✪ Visualise your wolf. When you can see him clearly in your mind's eye, say the following charm:

> *Mighty wolf, I honour thee*
> *And call you to this place.*
> *I ask that you protect me*
> *Within this time and space.*
> *Guard me close with tooth and claw;*
> *Shield me from all harm.*
> *Fear and fright I know no more;*
> *Your wolf strength keeps me calm.*
> *Snap and snarl at those who seem*
> *Intent on being my foe.*
> *Creature of my witchcraft dream,*
> *Protect me with your wolf patrol!*

Family bonding spell

Within the pack, wolves share a strong family bond. This spell will enhance your own family relationships.

What you need

A single strand of hair from each person in the family (this can be obtained from hairbrushes and combs), an envelope, a pen, a statue or picture of a wolf

What you do

- ✪ Take the hairs and twine them together.
- ✪ Put them in the envelope, seal it and write on it: 'To strengthen the pack'.
- ✪ Place the envelope beneath a wolf statue on your shrine, or secure it behind a wolf picture or in your Earth Shadows book.

Wild Hunt banishing spell

In witchcraft the Wild Hunt is a pack of phantom black hounds fronted by a rider on a ghostly black steed. In the Norse tradition this rider is Odin, while here in Britain he is generally believed to be Herne the Hunter. The Wild Hunt rides through the skies in the depths of the winter months, and most especially on 31 October – Halloween, or Samhain as witches call it. The Hunt can often be seen in the shapes of the winter storm clouds and can be called upon to remove any negative aspect of your life.

What you do

- ✪ Go outside on a stormy autumn or winter night, face the wind and rain, and tell Herne which aspect of your life you would like him to take away with him as he rides through the night, driving his pack before him.

To create a cunning plan

This simple spell calls on the fox and his naturally cunning ways.

What you need
A notepad and pen

What you do

⭐ Sit in your magical place with the notepad and pen close by. Bring to mind the image of a lovely red fox.

⭐ When you see the fox clearly, say:

> *Spirit of the cunning fox, I call on your skills. I ask that you inspire me with a cunning plan for —— (state your purpose) and lend me the wit and wisdom to carry it through. So mote it be!*

⭐ Remain in your magical place and jot down any ideas that come to mind. By weaving and linking these ideas together you should end up with a very foxy plan!

Fox and hound spell

If, like me, you abhor fox hunting (or any blood sport), then cast this little spell of protection as often as you can.

What you need
A picture or statue of a fox, a box of rock salt

What you do

⭐ Take the picture or statue of the fox and the rock salt to your altar. Place the fox in the middle of the altar and surround it with an unbroken circle of rock salt.

⭐ Chant this spell for as long as you can remain focused on the protection of foxes everywhere:

> *Fox and hound, fox and hound,*
> *May scent of fox never be found.*

Fox and hound, fox and hound,
Keep all foxes safe and sound.
So mote it be!

✪ Leave the fox image and the salt circle in place until after the hunt or for 24 hours and then clear away your things, scattering the rock salt on the winds.

Foxy lady spell

This one is for the ladies! No other creature is quite as slinky as the fox, so if you'd like a boost of confidence before a hot date, or simply to enhance your attractiveness and sex appeal, this fun spell just might turn you into a total vixen! You should wear red to perform it. Red, the colour of the fox, is equal to black for its effortless sexiness and will automatically get everyone's attention.

What you need
Your make-up – including eye-liner, mascara and red lipstick

What you do
✪ In your red outfit, sit before the mirror and apply your make-up. Pay particular attention to your eyes and try to make them as 'foxy' as possible, using eye-liner and mascara. Finally, add a slick of red lipstick and say the following spell three times:

Eyes across a crowded room
Turn and catch my gaze.
This spell I weave at the magic loom
To give me vixen ways.
Sexy, sultry, foxy lady,
Oozing sex appeal,
Slinky, feisty, shady lady,
Your heart I vow to steal.
Blinking, winking, stars are twinkling,
I'll take you to the moon.

Vixen thoughts are what I'm thinking.
Come now and grant my boon!

✪ For tonight you are now a vixen. The spirit of the fox is within you, so do her justice and have a great time!

To protect your dog

This spell will magically guard and protect your dog.

What you need
Your dog's collar, your pentacle, juniper or rosemary essential oil, a magical charm (optional)

What you do
✪ Place your dog's collar on your pentacle and leave it there for 24 hours.

✪ Anoint the collar with the juniper or rosemary essential oil, both renowned for their protective qualities. Make sure you only anoint the outside of the collar and not the part that lies next to your dog's skin, as neat essential oils can cause skin irritation.

✪ Once the oil has been absorbed, place the collar around your dog's neck, adding the magical charm if you wish.

Horse Power

Throughout the centuries the horse has given himself tirelessly in service to humankind. As a means of transport, as a soldier in war, as a worker on the land, the horse has been our constant companion, playing a leading role in our evolution and development. The modern world owes much to the past service of the horse – as is evinced in the fact that we still describe cars in terms of horse power. Even today, the horse is still called upon as a familiar, often in an unconscious way. How many of you have a horseshoe of some kind to bring you good luck? Or know someone who has? The horse also appears in the logos of many large companies. Most famous, perhaps, is the black horse adopted by a well-known bank. This logo is so popular that it has survived a merger with another bank. In a memorable advertising campaign some years ago, the bank used a horse called Kustos to represent its corporate image. The picture of Kustos galloping across green fields, his mane and tail flying, is one that many people still remember.

Horses may not be a common sight on the streets any more, but they continue to figure large in our consciousness on the racetrack. Every weekend millions of people bet their hard-earned cash on the speed and stamina of a horse, whether they can afford to or not! And some of these horses become celebrities in their own right, such as the triumphant Grand National winner Red Rum, the beautiful steeplechaser Desert Orchid, or the tragic Shergar – the most impressive Derby winner in British racing history, who was never seen again after his kidnapping.

Turning to the realms of mythological horses, the magnificent unicorn is still the emblem of Scotland, proudly upholding the Scottish flag. This image can be seen throughout Scotland, the unicorn often accompanied by the red lion rampant, the royal standard of the Scottish monarchy. Both the lion and the unicorn symbolise royalty, nobility, strength and valour, so they are the perfect representatives of the Scots, who are a very proud and independent people.

As you can see, the horse as a familiar is alive and kicking within the modern world.

If wishes were horses, beggars would ride ...

My own love affair with horses began when I was a little girl. For a while I admired them from afar. I had posters of horses in my bedroom and a collection of pottery horses on my windowsill, and I learnt how to sew show ring plaits into a mane and tail by studying a library book and practising on my Barbie horse! I bought pony magazines, and read all the 'Jackie' books and 'Jinny' books, as well as any other pony books I could lay my hands on. I cried and cheered my way through *Black Beauty* and galloped across the Australian outback with Thowra, the Silver Brumbie. I was, as everyone said, pony mad, and the day finally came, in my tenth year, when I went to riding school. My first ever ride was courtesy of a little grey mare called Lucy, who bolted full gallop across an open field, with me clinging on to the saddle for dear life. But that was it – I was hooked!

Regular lessons commenced, and I bounced my way through the difficulties of learning to post to the trot and sit to the canter. Galloping was great, mucking out was fun, grooming was therapeutic and jumping was ace!

I loved everything about horses and though I've been bitten, kicked, thrown, bolted with, cornered and stood on, my great passion for them has never diminished. I have worked as a groom in an equestrian centre, had my own pony, volunteered to ride crazy horses who had practically killed their owners and was once lucky enough to ride Red Kelpie, a famous show jumping horse who belonged to a top international show jumping star. Horses always have been, and always will be, a huge part of my life.

I'm sure that some of you out there will be able to relate entirely to much of the above. The horse craze gets into your blood and you never fully recover. And who would want to?!

70   HORSE POWER

But before others of you go flicking to the next chapter, let me tell you now that you do not need access to a stable yard or in-depth equestrian knowledge to work with the horse as a familiar. You can just as easily work with a spirit horse as with several hundred pounds' worth of horse flesh. Although there are spells in this chapter for those of you who do ride, there are also spells for those who have never sat in the saddle in your life and never intend to! But who knows? Maybe this chapter will introduce you to the horse bug and will lead you to discover a latent talent for equestrianism and a passion for horses you never knew you had!

Folklore and superstition

As humankind's relationship with the horse deepened, folklore and superstitions developed, many of which still hold sway today. There is a belief, for example, that making love within the boundaries of one of the many chalk horses carved into hillsides in England will increase the chance of conception. Disturbing dreams are said to be brought to us by the Night Mare, and the horseshoe is, of course, a famous lucky charm. But what were the origins of such beliefs, and what place, if any, do they have in modern magic and witchcraft? To answer this question we must delve into the depths of Celtic mythology.

To the ancient Celts the horse was a sacred animal, associated with the goddess Epona. Epona was a fertility deity, a mother goddess and a divine protector of equines. She was incredibly beautiful, as is proclaimed in the tale of Rhiannon, Epona's Welsh counterpart, and she could shape-shift into a beautiful white mare. It is believed that the hillside carvings of horses found in southern England were originally created in her honour – hence their association with fertility. Epona was so powerful a goddess that the Romans adopted her, calling on her to protect their cavalry steeds.

Epona, like many other gods and goddesses, also has a darker side, for she has been associated with the terrifying white Night Mare. Bear in mind, however, that even the most frightening of such visitations have something to teach us. By carefully analysing our nightmares, we can often come up with valuable insights into our life, so perhaps even this aspect of Epona is really a gift.

Horses are also sacred to several of the classical Greek and Roman gods, such as Mars, guardian of the war horse; Poseidon, associated with the white horses of the waves; and Helios, whose chariot was drawn by horses.

Blacksmiths

The blacksmith has long been held as something of a magician, summoning the elements and bending iron to his will in order to create useful and beautiful objects within the smoky realm of his forge. In many traditions he is associated with the dwarves, the elementals of Earth (also called gnomes), who dwell deep in underground caverns and within their forges craft magical swords that never know defeat.

In other traditions the blacksmith is linked to the elves, who dwell in woodland areas and are reputed to craft the finest silver work and weaponry. This is especially the case in the Norse tradition, where the King of Elves, Wayland or Volundr, is a god in his own right, as well as a highly magical and accomplished blacksmith. Wayland was the son of a sailor and a mermaid and was renowned for the magical artefacts he created, the most famous of all being a boat fashioned entirely from feathers.

Blacksmiths were also believed to be healers, both of horses and of humans. It was thought that the water the blacksmith used to cool the horseshoes absorbed his magic and could be used to cure all manner of ailments, such as deep battle wounds and broken bones. Drinking this water was thought to cure colic in a horse. British tradition has it that to carry a blacksmith's anvil for him will bring you great blessings for the rest of your life. I tried this once when I worked in the stables and nearly broke my back! I don't recommend it unless you are strong and hefty and slightly bigger than my five foot two inches. Personally, being a magical witch and all, I can happily forego such blessings as anvil-carrying may bring!

Horseshoes and harness

The horseshoe is probably the most popular good luck charm in our culture. Crafted using the elements by the magical blacksmith and worn by the sacred horse, it is believed to bestow good fortune and happiness on the household it protects. A horseshoe was also traditionally hung above the stable door to protect the horses within, as, according to an ancient legend, witches borrow horses in the night, ride them hard and then return them to the stable just before dawn, lathered up and exhausted. In this state they were known as 'hag-ridden' – as a horse-riding witch who is not remotely haggish and who would never steal a horse and ride it to exhaustion, I object strongly to this term!

Witches and wise women would themselves hang a horseshoe – sideways – on their door to identify themselves to people who might need their services. The sideways horseshoe represents the crescent moon and thus the Goddess. Needless to say, such ornamentation was swiftly removed during the Burning Times, and this tradition has all but died out. However, there are those in the know who still make use of it, so keep your eyes open.

Traditionally associated with gypsy horses and later with draught horses and cart horses, horse brasses also have a magical history. Crafted from brass, the metal of the sun, and fashioned into intricate shapes such as suns, moons, pentagrams, leaves, flowers, stars and hearts, they are far more than equine decoration; in fact, they are a symbolic protection device. Horse brasses are traditionally woven with red and white ribbons to invoke the mother goddess in the form of Epona and hung with bells to ward off negativity. Their association with good fortune and protection makes them a popular ornament in people's homes, particularly in farmhouses and country cottages. They are generally placed on either side of the fireplace – again making the link with the blacksmith and his element of fire.

The water kelpie

The water kelpie is a creature of folklore, said to resemble a black or grey horse. It appears to be quite harmless and is usually found grazing the lush grass that grows beside lochs, streams, rivers and lakes. The legend goes that if a person mounts such a creature, it will set off at full gallop and ride right into the depths of the water, thus drowning its unfortunate rider.

The phantom horse

In the darkness of the night the silence is broken by the eerie sound of galloping hooves ... Phantom horses are apparently haunting areas all over the British Isles. Some of these horses pull a ghostly carriage and carry headless passengers. Such a horse and carriage is said to carry Sir Thomas Boleyn, Anne Boleyn's father, who haunts the Norfolk countryside on the anniversary of his daughter's execution. One thing puzzles me, however; if this ghost is headless, how do people know who he is?

Thomas Hardy's classic novel, *Tess of the D'Urbervilles*, is allegedly based on the real-life legend of a ghostly coach and four that haunts the Turberville family in Dorset, warning them of impending disaster. Anyone who has read the book will know that the death of Tess Durbeyfield's horse marks the beginning of a tragic life for her.

A whole herd of headless white horses, thought to be old war horses of a battle long since past, are said to haunt the Hertfordshire countryside, while in areas of Sussex the sound of ghostly hooves is often heard at the witching hour. Other phantom horses are said to be joined in their hauntings by a great black dog, so it would seem that ghostly equines and old padfoot are the best of friends in the shadow world!

Tales of headless horsemen abound, many of whom are believed to be the ghosts of unfortunate highwaymen who were captured and brought to justice. Perhaps it was hearing of such a ghost that inspired American Washington Irving to write his famous tale *The Legend of Sleepy Hollow*.

If this area of folklore interests you, then visit a library or book store and study the legends. There are many tales of animal hauntings throughout Britain, and folklore regarding phantom horses is rich. It would seem that once darkness falls, the British countryside is a haven of ghostly activity for spectral horses. So who knows? There could be one near you!

Hobby horses

The hobby horse is far more than a child's toy. It has a past that is deeply rooted in pagan history. And hobby horses come in all sorts of shapes and forms, such as masks and costumes, as well as the 'head on a stick' variety we are all familiar with.

The beautiful county of Derbyshire is just a short drive from where I live. There, in the depths of a cavern called the Pin Hole Cave, is an ancient drawing of a man wearing the mask of a horse. This artwork dates back to the Stone Age, and illustrates that man and horse have shared a very long relationship and that the idea of the hobby horse is far from new. The first hobby horses as we know them were simply a stick or a branch with the skull of a horse attached to the top. These were carried as part of the Samhain and Yuletide festivals, which were important celebrations in the Old Religion. Indeed, they can still be seen today in some parts of Wales, Kent and Yorkshire.

There is a tradition of the hobby horse joyfully chasing young maidens, thus linking it with Epona and her gifts of fertility. In some areas, the hobby horse was ridden across the fields to ensure a bountiful crop. Riding the hobby horse also echoes the idea of witches flying on broomsticks, thought by some to have a sexual connotation. It is also said that young ladies who are taking sensible precautions against pregnancy would do well not to work with Epona too often and should never ride a hobby horse! You've been warned!

Horse whisperers

Horse whispering is the ability to calm even the wildest and most dangerous horse and get him to follow you as a foal follows his dam. Despite the popular assumption that it originated among gypsies and horse thieves, horse whispering is actually a very ancient art, possibly dating back to Roman times – though it is true that, for obvious reasons, it has historically been a skill highly prized by those with a desire to get their hands on horses illegally. In the days before sophisticated electronic security systems, if you could persuade a valuable stallion to follow you quietly of its own accord, you could be long gone by the time the alarm was raised. Not surprisingly, this gave rise to the belief that horses were spirited away in the night by witches.

The fact that many horse thieves came of gypsy stock and gypsies had a long association with magic and witchcraft, simple reinforced this popular belief.

Even in the modern world, whisperers are regarded with awe and superstition. Such skills can take years to learn. Most whisperers closely guard their secrets and will not tell just anyone how to go about it. There are various degrees of horse whispering, from the very basic to the truly exceptional. Someone like me – with knowledge and experience of horses and a few tricks up their sleeve – can walk up to a strange horse in a field and within a short time have him relaxed and docile. A tasty titbit can serve as an introduction and the rest is done through eye contact, voice and touch. In this state it would be easy to slip a head collar on him and lead him quietly away. But this is very basic horse whispering.

A true horse whisperer, and the most famous one of our time, is Monty Roberts, who tamed a wild mustang in a day and named him Shy Boy. If you have a horse or go riding and would like to learn a few whispering tricks, then do read his books, as they are completely fascinating to anyone with an interest in horses. And to watch Monty's videos is to learn from a master! Monty has vowed that his mission in life is to leave the world a better place – for the horse. Well, you can't argue with that!

Before we leave the subject of horse whispering I'd just like to add a quick word on the subject of 'breaking in'. This was the term used for many years for the practice of taming a horse and teaching him to accept saddle, bridle and rider or harness and cart. In days gone by, a horse really was broken in – his spirit was broken and he became a down-trodden servant (though in the process the horse-breaker would often risk life and limb). Because of its history and negative implications, 'breaking in' is not a term that I or any modern horsey people I know ever use. These days we 'start' a horse. Rather than breaking his spirit, we gently persuade him by nurturing his confidence, gaining his trust and allowing his wonderful spirit to work for us. This way we have the full co-operation and willingness of the horse. In my opinion, if you need whips and spurs to make a horse move, you shouldn't be sat on one in the first place. Enough said!

Equine psychology

In some ways the horse can be seen as humankind's greatest success story as far as domestication goes. The cat still maintains his independence, and – if in any way mistreated – the dog will occasionally turn and bite the hand that feeds him, but the horse? Well, the horse is just there, quietly grazing in his field, placid, tame and waiting patiently until the time when he is needed ... or is he?

Anyone who has ever been faced with the prospect of riding or handling a 'difficult' (read 'dangerous') horse will know that the horse is still wild at heart. And anyone who has ever been bolted with will know the truth of the phrase 'If a horse is gonna go, he's gonna go!'. The best that you can do in such a situation is pray to divinity and just hang on!

Perhaps one reason for the misconception that the horse has been completely mastered is that dogs and cats are carnivores and hunters, while the horse is a herbivore and therefore naturally more placid. This also means that while he is prey, we, as omnivores and hunter/gatherers, are his predators. His genetic instincts therefore warn him not to trust us – all the more amazing therefore that he will allow us to ride on his back. Understand this and you will understand the horse, for his entire behaviour pattern stems from the fact that he is a prey animal. Given time and observation, you will be able to predict his behaviour – a valuable skill when riding in busy traffic.

Due to the position of their eyes, horses have blind spots directly in front of and directly behind them, and they automatically fear what they cannot see clearly. They are creatures with a fight or flight mentality, but they will only fight if they have no alternative. In most situations, when a horse is frightened or nervous, his solution is to run for it!

A horse will flee until a distance of about 400 metres (437 yards) is between him and whatever has frightened him. Then he will turn to make sure that the nasty thing isn't pursuing him. However, when a horse has a rider on his back, his ability to flee is much hampered, and this can result in a horse prancing sideways and being generally skittish. Remember, too, that the horse has acute hearing and a great sense of smell, and he may have been frightened by something you are totally unaware of. Reassure him with pats and rubs and the soothing sound of your voice.

When introducing a horse to new things, such as a new item of tack or grooming kit, allow him to have a good look at it first. Let him sniff it and feel it with his muzzle, and allow him to become fully acquainted with the item before using it in your daily stable routine.

I once saw a horse go absolutely wild when his owner tried to throw a new reflective rug over him. The bright yellow colour totally freaked him out and, as he was confined to a loose box and couldn't flee, he made his objections known by squealing, rearing, bucking and kicking – in short he felt that he had no alternative but to fight. If his owner had introduced the rug gradually, maybe by hanging it over the stable door for a while, both she and her horse could have been spared a traumatic experience. Fortunately, neither one was hurt, but it's worth remembering that a frightened horse is a dangerous horse.

When faced with an aggressive horse, an old whispering trick is to stand tall and square and hold your arms out to the sides. Stand your ground and maintain eye contact with the horse. This can take some courage on your part, but eventually he will back off and will move away. Remember, you are the predator, he is the prey. His natural instinct is to avoid you, not attack you.

Another problem you may encounter while out riding out is noisy, snapping dogs. To a horse, strange dogs are simply wolves, and he will dance and kick out in order to keep the 'wolf' away from his vulnerable stomach region. This is the area that wolves attack in the wild. Although the dog is probably being friendly, it can be a harrowing experience for the horse. It can also be frustrating when the dog's owner says, 'It's okay, he won't bite', mistakenly assuming that this is your only dilemma and never guessing that you could end up with a bolting horse on your hands! If this happens, point out politely that your horse doesn't like strange dogs and has a habit of kicking out, and you don't want their dog to get hurt. Then watch how quickly the lead is snapped on and the dog led away to safety!

If you ride, I strongly suggest that you study equine psychology and modern horse whispering techniques as much as you can, as they will improve your riding and increase your communication with your horse. By acknowledging his natural instincts you will be able to anticipate his actions more accurately.

A shrine to the horse

The horse is a truly noble creature and we should honour him as such, for we will never be able to repay our debt to him for all that he has done for humankind throughout the course of history.

You could base your shrine on your own horse if you have one, using photos, rosettes and trophies you have won together, or you could dedicate it to the entire species, using pictures, statues and, of course, a lucky horseshoe!

Where the wild horses go ...

This is a meditation exercise, so you might like to create the appropriate atmosphere by lighting candles and incense. Remember also that your body temperature drops slightly during meditation, so turn the heating up a notch or put on a cosy jumper. You can either record the meditation text onto a tape and play it back to yourself or you can get a friend to read it to you. Whoever is reading, it should be done slowly, leaving plenty of gaps between sentences.

What you do

⚫ Make yourself comfortable and relaxed, either sitting or lying down, but making sure to keep your spine straight. Close your eyes.

⚫ Count slowly down from ten to one, concentrating on breathing deeply, in through your nose and out through your mouth. Once you are ready, turn on the tape or ask your friend to begin reading.

You are walking through a deep, dark forest, brushing aside the ferns and bending beneath the overhanging branches as you go. As you walk you hear the neighing and calling of a herd of wild horses in the distance. You move towards the sound.

As you do so you feel your consciousness changing, becoming less human and more equine. Your feet become hardened, and looking down you see hooves. Your spine lengthens and your

*limbs grow long and delicate. You are a horse and you scent the
air with your flaring nostrils. The breeze blows your mane and
ruffles your forelock as you pick your way through the trees,
following the scent and the sounds of the herd ahead.*

*As you come to the edge of the forest, a beautiful meadow of
lush green grass opens out before you. Your ears prick at the
sound of a stream gurgling in the distance and you survey the
scene before you. The wild herd are grazing at the far end of the
meadow and you lift your head and squeal out a joyful cry to
them. They whinny a welcome in answer, and you trot towards
them, feeling the springy grass beneath your hooves.*

*As you join the herd, a gentle mare comes up to welcome you,
blowing into your nostrils in greeting. She moves closer into your
space and begins to groom your shoulder with her teeth. It feels
good and you know that you have been accepted as one of the
herd. Eventually, you both dip your heads and begin to graze. The
grass is juicy and sweet and you graze your way over to the
stream. There you drink your fill and then step into the cool water
and allow it to wash over your hooves and around your fetlocks.*

*But now the herd is on the move and you gallop away with
them, feeling the strength of your limbs, your hooves pounding
and digging into the earth beneath you.*

*You run with the herd for as long as you wish and, when you
are ready, you detach from the wild horses and return to the
forest. The woodland is dark and shady, and as you walk
through it you become aware that you are once again shape-
shifting – this time back into your human form.*

✪ Once you are fully returned to your human body, count slowly
from one to ten and gently come out of your meditation.
Write down your thoughts and feelings and what you learnt
during your meditation in your book of Earth Shadows.

To bless a lucky horseshoe

What you need
Your horseshoe, spring water (bottled is fine), sea salt

What you do
⭐ Take your horseshoe to your altar and sprinkle it with a mixture of the spring water and sea salt. Then bless it with the following words:

> *Shoe of iron, forged in fire,*
> *Epona hear my desire.*
> *I hold before me a magic charm*
> *To protect me from all forms of harm.*
> *Worn on the hoof of the sacred horse,*
> *It will bring good luck as a matter of course.*
> *So mote it be!*

⭐ Place the horseshoe on your horse shrine if you have one, or hang it above your door, points up to enjoy its luck-bringing qualities or points sideways to make a statement about your pagan beliefs!

To call a spirit horse

If you would like to work with horses as a familiar but do not have one of your own, then call a spirit horse. You can focus on your spirit horse for many of the spells in this chapter by calling him into the Circle using the invocation on page 82.

Before you call your horse, you will need to decide what he looks like. What colour is he? How big is he? What markings does he have – dapples, star, stockings, socks, blaze, snip? Is he of a particular breed? What is his temperament – feisty but faithful or gentle and confident? What age and gender is your spirit horse – a stallion, a gelding, a mare, a filly a colt? Once you have a clear picture of your spirit horse in your mind, keep your eyes peeled for a picture or statue that looks just like him and beg or buy it. If you can't find a picture or statue, you can call your spirit horse using the picture in your head.

What you need
A picture or statue of your spirit horse (optional), two candles, matches or a lighter

What you do
- ✪ If you are using a picture or statue of your spirit horse, place it on your horse shrine. Otherwise, conjure up the image of your spirit horse in your head.
- ✪ Light two candles on your horse shrine, on either side of the picture or statue of your spirit horse if you are using one. Now call your horse in the following way:

> *I send my voice on the spirit winds*
> *A spirit horse here to bring.*
> *Sacred equine hear my cry;*
> *Together we will gallop and fly.*
> *The wind in your mane, the wind in my hair,*
> *A magical bond of trust we share.*
> *I offer my love to all your kind*
> *And bring my spirit horse to mind.*

White horses summoning spell

For this spell you will need to be on a beach during an incoming tide, for it calls on the power of the white horses of the waves to bring your desire.

What you do
- ✪ Stand on the seashore and focus on the waves as they come in. Be sure that the tide is coming in so that the magical energy is right to bring something your way.
- ✪ Visualise your main goal, clearly imagining what it is you

want. Holding this vision in your mind, begin to chant the following charm:

> *White horses on a wild sea,*
> *I send this spell through time.*
> *Carry my wish forth to me;*
> *Bring what I have in mind.*
> *Grant my desire through time and space;*
> *My dreams on white horses ride.*
> *Here and now my magic takes place*
> *With the power and the strength of the tide.*

★ Continue to recite the words of the spell until the waves cast a white pebble or shell at your feet. Pick up this gift and take it as a sign that your wish has been heard. Place the pebble on your horse shrine. Your spell will manifest in due course.

To overcome obstacles

You can work this spell with a real horse or by envisioning yourself riding your spirit horse. If you are working with a real horse, you need to be a fully competent rider, as you will have to jump fences.

What you do

★ If you are working with a real horse, go to a place where there are fences you can jump safely.

★ Whether your horse and fence are real or visionary, spend some time visualising the fence as the obstacle you wish to overcome. For example, the fence could represent ill health or financial difficulty.

★ Keeping this image firmly in your mind, jump over the fence. If you are working with a spirit horse, you can envision yourself jumping the same fence over and over again. With a real horse, however, you will need a varied course, so remember to visualise the obstacle with each new fence you jump.

⭐ Repeat this exercise daily until you have overcome the obstacle in your life.

For stamina

This spell is for situations in which you feel you need increased stamina – a sporting event you are taking part in, for instance.

What you need
A candle, matches or a lighter

What you do
⭐ Go to your horse shrine, light a candle and say:

> *I take into myself the strength and stamina of the horse. May equine energy surround me and uphold me. Blessed be!*

⭐ Allow the candle to burn down. (For safety's sake, stay in the room while this is happening.)

To challenge someone

This spell calls on the power of stallions, who regularly challenge one another for mating rights over the herd. You can use the spell in any situation in which you feel you must challenge someone – their motives, their actions, their leadership and so on. For the best results, memorise the spell.

⭐ Just prior to your challenge, repeat this spell three times:

> *Mighty stallion, I summon you. I honour your courage, your nobility, your strength. I ask that these attributes surround me and assist me in the challenge I am about to make. May the strength and courage of the stallion reside in me and guide me through the battle ahead, and may I become the reigning stallion. So mote it be!*

To protect horses

What you need
Some candles and incense

What you do

✪ Go to your horse shrine, light the candles and incense, and sit before it. Now repeat this chant for as long as you are able to stay focused:

Blessed be Epona, and all her equine charges!

To protect your equine tools

If you own a horse, this little witch trick will help you to keep your tack, rugs, grooming kit and so on safe from thieves.

What you need
An essential oil of protection (such as rosemary or lavender), a silver pentagram, 3 yew twigs

What you do

✪ Using the oil of protection, mark each of your tools with a pentagram. When marking your tack, make sure you put the oil on an area that does not touch the horse's skin, as essential oils can be skin irritants.

✪ Hang the silver pentagram on your bridle, from the side of the brow band. This will also protect your horse when he is wearing it.

✪ When you have marked every item in your grooming kit, place the three yew twigs in your tack box. The yew is a tree of strong protective magic. Support this spell by locking all your tools away safely when they are not in use.

To protect your horse from theft

What you need
A photograph of your horse, an envelope, 3 sprigs of lavender, 3 pinches of dried basil, a pen

What you do

- First of all, make sure your horse is properly freeze marked. Then write the freeze mark on the back of the photo.
- Place the photo in the envelope, together with the lavender and basil, both of which are herbs of protection. Then seal the envelope and write on it:

    Protected by witchcraft.
    Protected by me.
    Protected be!

Woodland Ways

In this chapter we will be looking at the creatures that inhabit a typical English woodland. We will be exploring the magic of rabbits, squirrels, moles, hedgehogs, deer and so on, and looking at what kinds of magic these particular familiars can assist us with. Britain has a wealth of wildlife just waiting to be discovered, and as witches we can tap into the energies of specific animals to aid us in our spell-castings.

The wildwood witch

'Wildwood' is a pagan term that refers to the primitive energies of the trees and the surrounding woodland. A wildwood is a place that emanates magic and power, and many witches choose such a place for working their outdoor rituals. Any woodland can be a wildwood; you simply have to attune with the magic of the land and the power of the trees and perform your basic rituals there, thus adding to the aura of power. The ritual can be as quick and simple as burning a stick of incense as you meditate beneath a tree or as complex as gathering with a group of like-minded friends to perform seasonal magic (see my book *The Witch's Almanac 2004* for more information on seasonal spells).

A wildwood witch has a close connection with the local woodlands around her, many of which are survivors of the great forest that once stretched from London to the far north of England. This forest was home to many creatures, the best-known being herds of the King's deer. To become a wildwood witch spend as much time as you possibly can in your local woodland. Visit it in all seasons, seeing the trees in their many outfits – spring blossom, summer leaf, autumnal hues and the frosts and snows of winter. Get to know the land and the animals that live there, and work with traditional woodland animals as familiars. Make a note of what you observe and the magic you perform in your Earth Shadows book.

The woodland shrine

A shrine created to reflect the magic of the woodland can be very beautiful and is a magical way to bring the essence of the wildwood into your home. You can let your imagination run wild if you want to, as there are lots of lovely things that have a place on such a shrine. Pictures of trees can be hung above your shrine, and a large leafy plant could be placed nearby. Candles placed in tree-like candlesticks, or tea-lights in leaf-shaped holders would be very appropriate, as would little statues of woodland creatures. In the middle you could place a figure or picture to represent one of the guardians of the woods, for example, Robin Hood, Sadb the deer goddess (see page 24) or a woodland sorceress. Add to this the gifts of nature, such as pine cones, acorns and fresh blackberries picked from the hedgerow and your shrine is complete.

Deer and stags

Deer can be found throughout most of Britain and are particularly common in the Highlands of Scotland. They have long been hunted as a source of food, although in the past this was a privilege only those of noble blood could partake of. Any commoner found hunting 'the King's deer' would risk the loss of a hand – the standard punishment for breaking the Law of Venison.

Deer and stags hold a key place in Celtic mythology. By the Celts they were considered to be sacred creatures. In many stories a Celtic hero hunts the white hart, a deer of purest white. The white hart is said to be a messenger from the Otherworld, so take careful note if one appears in your dreams. Many gods and goddesses are associated with the deer, among them Apollo, Arawn, Cernnunos, Diana, Artemis, Nemesis and Britomart. In English folklore the deer is strongly associated with Robin Hood and Herne the Hunter, both of whom are aspects of the pagan god.

Herne the Hunter is said still to haunt Windsor Great Park. He is one of the gods believed to lead the Wild Hunt through the winter months, riding a phantom black horse and driving a pack of whisht hounds before him. In appearance he resembles a tall, strong man with long untamed hair and wild eyes. Antlers grow from his brow, and he carries a hunting horn and wears delicate chains strung with tiny silver bells on his sleeves. He is the masculine spirit of paganism, and magical practitioners can attune with him via the stag.

A close look at a stag will reveal a creature of stature and strength, with an almost equine grace about him. Like the horse, the stag has a long arched neck, powerful, slender legs and the ability to take flight at a moment's notice. But there the similarity ends, for the stag has a fey quality that is very un-equine and rather Otherworldly. The sight of a herd of deer running freely is quite magical and awe-inspiring. They teach us that power and majesty can go hand in hand with grace and humility.

Stags and deer tend to graze at the hours of dawn and dusk, the time when the veil between our world and the Otherworld is thin. They are also associated with winter, the season when we are closest to the Otherworld and when magic is afoot. Not for nothing is Santa's sleigh pulled by reindeer. He visits this world by magic on one night of the year and then hastens away to his winter realm. This has led to the belief that stags and deer can slip easily from our world into the shadow lands and back again, making them excellent messengers, and a great vehicle for connecting with the deities associated with them.

To attune with Herne

If you feel an affinity with Herne, then work this ritual to call on his energies. This spell can be performed prior to a meditation, or just before working with any familiar, particularly those in this chapter. You could also use this spell as a simple protection rite.

What you do

- ✪ Go to a woodland in your area, or stand beneath a tree – the oak is especially sacred to Herne.

- ✪ Relax and bring to mind the image of a magnificent stag. He has huge antlers spreading out over his brow and he stands quietly before you, his large brown eyes meeting your gaze without fear.
- ✪ Once you can visualise the stag clearly, repeat the following spell, either out loud or in your head:

> *The secrets of natural magic I wish to learn,*
> *So I come to the wildwood and call on Herne.*
> *Mighty stag of seven tines,*
> *Connect me with Herne in this magical time.*
> *As a sacred messenger I send you now*
> *To bring forth the god with the antlered brow.*
> *So mote it be!*

- ✪ In your mind's eye see the stag dip his head in acquiescence and then turn and run through the woods. He disappears from sight and you know that he has gone to the Otherworld to fetch Herne.
- ✪ Wait for a few moments and then again use your visualisation skills, this time to bring Herne into being. See him walking through the trees towards you, dressed in shades of green and brown, the antlers upon his brow standing tall and strong. As he walks you hear the tinkling sound of the silver bells he wears – a sign of his connection with the Goddess. He stands before you and smiles down upon you.
- ✪ Finish the spell by telling Herne how you wish him to assist you in your magic – helping you better to understand animals, for example, or protecting and guiding you in your daily life. Know that Herne's energy and power will begin to permeate your life and then see the vision fade before you. Continue your walk through the wildwood or return home.

Shrine to the stag

Another way to connect with Herne, or with the stag as a power animal, is to set up a shrine within your home dedicated to stags and deer. Any posters, paintings or figures of stags can be used – if you wait until November or December to create this shrine, you will find that you are spoilt for choice.

Yuletide is the sabbat most closely associated with the stag and this association has been carried over into modern-day Christmas celebrations. Stags, deer and reindeer are everywhere at this time of year. You may find stag-shaped candleholders, ornaments, stained glass sun-catchers and many other items. A lot of these decorations have no reference to Christmas on them – they are simply stags placed in snowy settings and so are ideal for a power animal shrine. Look in garden centres too, as you may find a lovely stag in the winter sale.

Remember to be adventurous with all your shrines and to make them personal to you. For instance, I love winter, so many of my altar decorations reflect this season. For example, I have a lovely snow angel figure sat in a swan-shaped sleigh, being drawn by a white heart stag. Such things are available if you look for them and are perfect for a magical shrine or altar. Keep your eyes peeled and see what you can find. Make your shrine represent not only the stag but also yourself.

Rabbits

Rabbits were brought to Britain by the Romans and are now a well established inhabitant of our countryside. During the Middle Ages they were kept as a source of food and were known as conies. To witches and followers of the Old Religion, the rabbit has always been a magical ally. For a time, rabbits were considered to be luck-bringers. There is a tradition in some areas of the British Isles that saying the word 'rabbits' three times on the first morning of every month with an 'R' in it will bring good fortune throughout that month. Up until the Middle Ages many people carried a rabbit's foot as a charm against evil. During the Burning Times, however, the rabbit became associated with witches and witchcraft. Such charms came to be viewed by many as cursed and were believed instead to bring about a run of bad luck. It was said that to relieve this bad luck the rabbit's foot had to be buried at a cross-roads. Poachers, however, hung on to their rabbit's foot, as it was believed that it would keep them from getting caught!

Rabbits are, of course, renowned for their incredible fertility – litters of up to seven young can be produced every four weeks! The leverets are born without fur and their eyes are tightly closed. (In this respect the rabbit is very different from its cousin, the hare, as hare leverets are born with a full fur coat and their eyes wide open.) Rabbit energy can be called upon to aid in the fertility of a garden, a project or a business venture, or, of course, the successful conception of a child.

Rabbit fertility spell

What you need
An image of a rabbit, incense (optional)

What you do
- ✪ Take the image of the rabbit to your altar and light the candles there. Also light incense if you wish. Focus on the rabbit and think clearly of fertility and healthy growth in your chosen area.
- ✪ Chant the following charm for as long as you can stay focused:

> *Rabbit, rabbit come to me;*
> *Bring your gift of fertility.*
> *Rabbit, rabbit come to me;*
> *Success in this venture I shall see!*

Squirrel

The red squirrel is native to Britain, but with the introduction of the North American grey squirrel in the late nineteenth century, it lost much of its territory. It is now extinct in most of England and is a common sight only in Scotland. Grey squirrels, however, are easy to spot throughout England. Both species are beautiful creatures in their own right.

Squirrels – both red and grey – make their nests, or dreys, high up in the trees, safe from predators. Contrary to popular belief, they do not actually hibernate as such, as they cannot go without food for more than two or three days at a time, but they do stock up larders of nuts and seeds within their dreys. This means that they have little reason to leave the nest during the winter and are therefore less active and more reclusive. Like many other creatures, squirrels spend more time sleeping during the winter, conserving their energy to be used as heat in these cold months.

The squirrel is sacred to the Scandinavian god Thor, who used this nimble creature as a messenger. The squirrel would move up and down the World Tree, Yggdrasil, carrying the word of Thor to any of its various inhabitants, from the eagle perched on the topmost branch to the snake guarding the roots.

We can call on squirrel energies to assist us with our finances, making magical use of this animal's hoarding instincts.

Squirrel savings spell

What you need
A pouch of nuts, seeds and grains

What you do
- ✪ Go to a wooded area where squirrels live, taking with you the pouch of nuts, seeds and grains as an offering.
- ✪ Sit quietly beneath a tree and in your mind repeat the following spell three times:

> *Squirrel scurrying here and there,*
> *Make my savings grow.*

Banish from me financial care;
Protect me from financial woe.
Squirrel hoarding nuts and seeds,
Hear the words I say.
Help me meet financial needs,
As with pounds and pence I line my drey.
So mote it be!

✪ Empty the offering pouch on the forest floor as a gift to the squirrels and, whenever you make a deposit into your savings account, visualise a squirrel running off with your cash and adding it to a pile of gold.

Moles

Moles are small creatures that live underground in a series of inter-connected tunnels, which they dig themselves. Although not completely blind as many people think, the mole does have very poor eyesight. However, when digging out his home he can detect traces of light from the world above, which he uses to direct him in his tunnel-building. Due to their underground existence, moles can be very elusive. Often the only sign of them is the little mole hills they leave behind. But even the smallest and seemingly most insignificant creature can be called upon as a magical ally and familiar.

To see light at the end of the tunnel

We all go through bad times and find ourselves in situations where we feel as if there is no light in our lives. If you are currently experiencing feelings like this, first of all try not to panic and do not allow yourself to become too depressed, as this will not help you to change things. Instead, do a little work with the familiar who knows all about darkness. Ask the mole to guide you forth from the underground and up into the light.

What you do

⭐ As darkness falls, go to your woodland shrine, or simply step out into your garden, and make this magical plea for assistance:

> *Little mole in darkness black,*
> *I cannot find my way.*
> *Clear my path, let joy come back;*
> *Guide me to the light of day.*
> *So mote it be!*

⭐ Repeat this spell on a daily basis until your life is filled with sunshine again.

To get to the bottom of a situation

The mole can also help us to get to the bottom of things when a situation is unclear or puzzling. Remember, though, that with this as with any other kind of truth spell, you may not like what is revealed, so be prepared.

What you do

⭐ Once again, go either to your woodland shrine or out into your garden as dusk begins to fall. Focus strongly on the situation that is puzzling you and say the following spell nine times:

> *Little mole dig down deep;*
> *Leave no stone unturned.*
> *From me the facts they cannot keep;*
> *The truth now I shall learn.*
> *By the power of three times three,*
> *This is my will. So shall it be!*

Hedgehogs

A couple of summers ago there was a hedgehog living at the bottom of my garden. I struck up quite a friendship with him and eventually named him Puck. The nicest thing about Puck, who was only a baby, was that he would turn up, make a loud snuffling noise and then wait until I brought him a little plate of cat food, which he loved! Supper over, he would make his way back to his cosy nest of leaves in the roots of the tall poplar trees, and would settle down quite happily.

The hedgehog is widespread throughout Britain and is one of the sacred animals of the Goddess. It is also associated with faeries – in fact, it is often said that a hedgehog is really a faerie in disguise! Like many creatures strongly linked with witchcraft, the hedgehog has been deemed both good and evil at different times and by different people.

Apart from human beings, hedgehogs are the only creatures on Earth who can contract leprosy. This fact reinforced the popular belief that hedgehogs were really witches who had shape-shifted. It also meant that hedgehog spines were used in various 'cures' for the disease. In the past hedgehog spines were also used to lance boils and to card wool.

Hedgehogs are most active at dawn and dusk. They make their nests in dried leaves and twigs and spend the winter in hibernation. The hedgehog is best known for its incredible defence mechanism. By rolling into a tight little ball it presents only its spines to the world, and thus is safe from predators. The hedgehog's main downfall is the heavy traffic that travels up and down roads across the country.

Working with the hedgehog as a familiar can help you to develop your prickles, keeping them sharp and thus remaining somewhat protected from life's knocks.

To be prickly

There are occasions in life when it serves us well to become a little bit prickly! By hiding our softer side and our true gentle nature behind a shield of spines, we can protect ourselves from a certain amount of hurt and upset. Most people will be put off by such prickles, although those who take the time to look beyond the defensiveness and see our true nature will actually stick around – this is a great way to discover a true friend! Being a little bit prickly can also protect us in the work place or in any area where we are forced to interact with people we wouldn't normally choose to mix with, for whatever reason.

What you need
A picture or statue of a hedgehog (or a real hedgehog visitor to your garden)

What you do

✪ Focus your attention on the hedgehog picture or statue, or wait for your garden hedgehogs to emerge. Concentrating on your hedgehog, speak the following words:

> *Creature of the Goddess, I honour you. I call on your energies, for I have need of your power. Lend me your gift of protection and defensiveness. Let none irritate me or do me harm. Help me to keep my prickles newly sharpened that I may be safe throughout the trials of life. So mote it be!*

✪ Repeat this spell whenever you feel you need a little extra power to your natural defences.

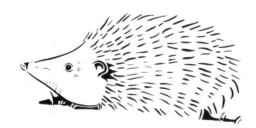

Mouse

Mice are sacred to the god Apollo and are symbolic of the abundance of the harvest. An old wives' tale states that to place a child's milk teeth within a mouse hole will ensure that the adult teeth grow strong and white. To the Egyptians, mice represented the fertility of all life. In Germany to see a white mouse was said to be incredibly lucky and was an omen of immense good fortune ahead. To dream of mice means that you have hidden enemies, while to dream of a single mouse indicates that a close friend or family member could be deceiving you in some way.

As a familiar the mouse can teach us to keep a low profile and go unnoticed during those times when we would prefer to be left alone.

To go unnoticed

What you need
Your mice, if you keep these animals as pets, or a picture or statue of a mouse

What you do
✦ Either bring your mice, in their cage, to the altar or focus on the picture or statue of the mouse. Chant the following charm for as long as your focus remains strong and clear:

> Silently creeping,
> Softly cheeping,
> Quiet as a little mouse.
> As I fade from the scene,
> Don't wish to be seen,
> Unnoticed as a little mouse.
> So mote it be!

Creatures of the Night

Nocturnal animals and creatures associated with the moon have long been linked with magic and witchcraft. These are animals that have often been misunderstood, but they all have something to teach the witch and magical practitioner – whether it be the wisdom of the owl, the love of darkness of the bat or the resilience of the rat. A true witch is willing to learn from all of these animals and can see the beauty in them. In this chapter we will be exploring the magic and mystery of the creatures of the night.

Badgers

The badger, known to country folk as Old Brock, provides a link between the wildwood and the realm of night. Badgers are often referred to as 'the oldest land owners in Britain', as they have inhabited this island for so long. They tend to live in woodland areas, creating a series of underground tunnels and chambers known as setts, which they continually improve and 'renovate', before handing the homestead on to the younger generations of their bloodline. They come above ground to feed but, as they are strictly nocturnal animals, they can be quite elusive.

Due to deforestation, many badgers are now forced to live in close proximity with humans, and can occasionally be seen wandering through back gardens. My brother has a whole family of badgers that regularly visit his garden late at night to feed on the kitchen scraps left out for them. (My sister-in-law is a chef, and it is my belief that these may well be the best-fed badgers in Britain!) The first time I witnessed this I was amazed at the size of the badgers – they were much bigger than I had ever imagined them to be. Their distinctive black and white faces and ghostly silver grey bodies mean that they are actually quite easily seen, even at night. As animals who live underground they do not have a land creature's need for camouflage.

In Scotland, badger sporrans were once worn to invoke the warrior spirit – for badgers are true heroes who will fight regardless of how out-numbered, hampered or injured they are. I myself have seen a Scotsman in full Highland costume wearing a badger sporran, though at the time I was unaware of its significance. And in all fairness to the Scot, the sporran did look old, as though it had been handed down through the generations of his clan. It is highly unlikely that such sporrans are still being made, as the badger is now a protected species throughout Britain. However, this tradition does illustrate the fact that badgers have been called upon as a familiar for many, many years.

The despicable practice of badger baiting shows humanity at its worst and the badger at his best, for the same warrior spirit that the Celts once called upon in battle is sickeningly exploited by the baiters. If you ever hear of baiting in your area, do not confront the baiters yourself. Inform the police of all you know immediately, as badger baiting is illegal. Then inform your local RSPCA. Let the authorities deal with these people and then work the spell on the next page. Also, if you know the location of badgers and their sett, be sure to tell no-one and help to keep the badgers safe.

CREATURES OF THE NIGHT

To protect badgers from baiters

What you need

Matches or a lighter, a picture or statue of a badger, 4 quartz crystals, a slip of card, a black marker pen, some black paint or nail varnish, some thread or ribbon

What you do

✪ Take all the items to your altar and light the illuminator candles. Place your representation of a badger in the centre of your altar and surround it with the crystals, placing them at the four compass points and saying the words 'Protected be!' as you place each one. This will help to magically protect the badger on all sides.

✪ Using the marker pen, write the word 'baiters' on the slip of card, then paint both sides of the card black, blotting out the writing completely.

✪ Once the paint has dried, wrap the thread or ribbon around the card, pulling it tight and saying the following charm three times:

> *Bind the baiters, bind them tight;*
> *Keep the badgers from their sight.*
> *Stop the baiters inflicting pain;*
> *Prevent them doing harm again.*
> *Keep the badgers safe and sound;*
> *I weave the binding round and round.*
> *Keep the badgers from their sight;*
> *I send this spell on beams of light.*
> *So mote it be!*

✪ To complete the spell, tie off the thread, bury the card in the earth and leave the badger representation and crystals in place for three days and nights.

To invoke the warrior spirit

What you need
A black candle, a white candle, matches or a lighter, a statue or picture
of a badger

What you do

- Take the candles and statue or picture of the badger to your altar. Light the two candles and place the badger between them.
- Close your eyes and bring to mind the image of a strong yet gentle badger. Repeat the following charm three times:

> *Creature of the stripy face,*
> *Your warrior spirit I now embrace,*
> *Your strength and courage now I show*
> *That I may vanquish all my foes.*
> *Challenged, outnumbered I may be,*
> *With your gifts they'll not defeat me.*
> *Brock the badger, badger Brock,*
> *My trust in you they will not rock.*
> *Be with me and face my foe;*
> *Badger strength I now will know.*
> *So mote it be!*

Rats

Pest, vermin, grain thief, plague-bringer ... Just what, if anything, can the rat teach today's magical practitioner?

The human race has never really forgiven the rat for distributing the plague so efficiently among us! But let's make one thing clear right from the start – it was fleas living in the coats of the rats rather than the rats themselves that carried the plague. Hair-splitting? Well, not if you want to work with the rat as a familiar! Rats, like witches, have had a very bad press, and I am not going to add to it. Instead I will try to show you the sacredness of the rat and its magical uses.

In ancient times the rat was the sacred animal of Persephone, the Queen of the Underworld. Thus its connection with death long predates its association with the Black Death (c. 1348) and the Great Plague (c. 1665). Rats were also closely associated with the Celtic god Cernunnos, and in ancient Egypt they were symbolic of great spiritual wisdom.

In the wild, rats are extremely adaptable and can live almost anywhere, from houses, to fields, to sewers, to woodlands and even to ships, where they would sustain themselves by eating soap and candlewax when food was scarce! Rats reputedly have the same IQ as a dog. This intelligence, coupled with their agility and the prejudice most people feel against them, has unfortunately made them prime material for research laboratories. To others, though, they are much loved pets and companions. One of my friends keeps a couple of fancy rats. They are the most fascinating and adorable creatures, each with its own distinctive personality. They have long, silky whiskers and twitchy pink noses, and like nothing better than to run up sleeves or nibble at special ratty chocolate drops!

But perhaps the best quality of the rat is its resilience. In vain has humankind attempted to rid the world of rats. Still they thrive, building up an immunity to our poisons, working out escape routes from our traps and regarding our hatred with disdain! You have to hand it to them – such small and seemingly inferior creatures, but they have been known to make ladies faint and grown men scream, and have twice been the vehicle that has brought the world to its knees. The lesson? Never underestimate a rat!

To overcome hatred

No other creature on earth has suffered from quite such overwhelming hatred and discrimination as the rat. If you feel that you are up against similar challenges in life, try this spell. You can memorise the charm and use it to call on the rat as a familiar whenever you need to invoke his resilience and knack for survival against the odds.

What you need
A white candle, matches or a lighter

What you do

⭐ Light the candle and then focus on a mental image of a rat. Once you can see your rat clearly, call for his assistance in the following way:

> *Hurry, scurry, here and there;*
> *We're not wanted anywhere.*
> *Rat be nimble, rat be quick,*
> *Hear now my witchcraft trick.*
> *Teach me how to rise above*
> *Hatred and a lack of love.*
> *Teach me how to go my way*
> *Regardless of the things they say.*
> *Resilience is such a gift;*
> *I feel my spirits begin to lift.*
> *Resilience is your gift to me.*
> *Sacred rat, blessed be!*

Owls

The idea of an owl as a familiar has been popularised by J K Rowling's creation of Hedwig in the Harry Potter books. But owls have been linked to magic and witchcraft for centuries. Like the rat, the owl was believed to be an omen of death and a prophet of woe. He was regarded with suspicion during the Middle Ages, and magical people still consider it to be unlucky to see a wild owl flying during the day.

In mythology, owls are associated with the beautiful and bewitching sirens, who were a type of magical seductress. Owls are also the sacred birds of the goddesses Athene, Hecate, Guinevere and the Cailleach.

The first cry of an owl in November heralds the beginning of winter in the British Isles. While we generally associate owls with the ghostly too-whit-too-woo, the barn owl's cry is actually an unmistakeable screech. Several years ago, I was lying in bed reading a book when I heard this sound outside my window. I can remember jumping out of my skin at the noise. At first I didn't realise what it was, as I live on the edge of a large city and owls are not the first thing that spring to mind when you are confronted with a strange noise in the night! I got out of bed and went to look through the window. Just at that moment, a large owl flew by and let out another unearthly shriek. It was quite eerie, but also quite beautiful. I felt very privileged to have seen and heard such a magical creature, especially as it was so late and everyone else was fast asleep. It was as if the owl and I had shared a secret.

Due to their silent, gliding flight, owls are often likened to ghosts. Soundless as a spectre, they descend on their prey from behind. In some areas of Britain, dusk is referred to as 'owl light'. Owls have also been linked with healing. Soup made from their eggs was long thought to cure epilepsy, and owl eggs have also been used in morning-after cures for hangovers!

As a magical familiar, the owl can teach us about the dark side of life – night, winter, old age, death and rebirth – and, of course, about wisdom, magic and spell-casting.

A spell for wisdom

What you do

- Go to a dark outdoor place just before the witching hour. (If you are going away from home, take sensible safety precautions for being out on a dark night – and remember that this spell will work just as well in your own back garden.) As midnight strikes, call to mind the image of an owl and say the following words three times:

> *Hunting bird of ghostly flight,*
> *Hear the plea I make this night.*
> *Teach me all I need to know,*
> *And let my inner wisdom grow.*

To increase your magical ability

This spell will give you a magical boost of owl power

What you do

- As in the previous spell, go to a dark outdoor place just before the witching hour. This could be your garden or it could be somewhere else (in which case, take care of your own safety). As midnight strikes, visualise an owl clearly in your mind and repeat the following charm:

> *Here I stand at the witching hour*
> *To improve and increase my magical power.*
> *Owl of wisdom, magic and spell,*
> *Witchcraft secrets now you tell.*
> *I know so little – I would learn more,*
> *And be a witch to my very core.*
> *Sacred bird of magical power,*
> *Bring me your gifts in this witching hour!*

- Return home and go directly to bed. Make a careful note of your dreams for the next few nights, as the owl may send you a message.

Bats

There are many different species of bat, some of which are widespread throughout Britain. Bats roost in caves, ruined buildings and the hollows of trees. In general they prefer to keep away from human activity. They are nocturnal creatures, though occasionally during the warmer months of summer, they emerge at dusk rather than waiting until full darkness falls. In winter most species go into full or semi-hibernation. Bats feed on small flying insects, spiders and occasionally berries. It is only the notorious vampire bat that feeds on the blood of animals, and this particular species is not native to Britain.

The country name for the bat is 'flitter mouse', and, unlike birds, bats do have quite an erratic flight path. They are the only mammal with the power of true flight. Although bats are not completely blind, as is often supposed, their eyesight is extremely poor, and they rely for orientation on a type of sound radar known as sonar, generating high-pitched squeals that bounce back off obstacles, enabling the bat to avoid them during flight. In folklore it is said that if a bat flies into a building it is a sure sign of rain, Young bats are able to fly at just three weeks old.

Due to its nocturnal nature and its avoidance of human activity, the bat has been linked to loneliness and isolation, winter, night time, and, of course, the darker aspects of life. To those schooled in the lore of magic, however, darkness does not correspond with evil; it is simply another expression of nature's energy. The bat's association with darkness has been distorted and exaggerated by the makers of horror movies; as a result, the bat will forever be linked to the vampire in people's minds. But more on that later.

As a familiar, the bat can teach us the beauty and a joy of voluntary isolation – that we sometimes need to take ourselves away from the mundane activities of life in order to give ourselves quality time, by ourselves, for ourselves. The bat can also teach us to look at life from a fresh angle, as he does when he hangs upside down to roost. But perhaps the most useful life skill the bat has to offer is that of avoiding the obstacles that we find in our path.

To avoid obstacles

What you do

- Lie on your bed with your head hanging over the side, giving you a semi-upside-down view of the room. This may seem a little silly, but it will enable you to link your consciousness with that of the bat.

- Visualise the bat in your mind, first hanging upside down in his roost, then spreading his wings and taking flight, to emerge from the roost into the starry night sky. See how he flies, avoiding all the obstacles in his path, hunting his prey of moths and so on as he goes.

- Once you have this scene clear in your mind's eye, repeat the following spell three times:

> *Flitter mouse, flitter mouse,*
> *Guide me to where I want to go.*
> *Fly the starry sky so high;*
> *To me, my path you now will show.*
> *Help me to avoid the blocks,*
> *The obstacles within my way.*
> *Guide me on my path this night;*
> *Let success come with the break of day.*

- Continue the visualisation for as long as you wish, and know that the bat's energy will help you to avoid any blocks that may lie in your way.

Vampires

Of course, vampires are not really beasts, as they exist only in folklore, but I felt that I should stretch the point as they do form a fascinating part of any discussion of creatures of the night and have captured the human imagination for centuries.

Vampires are generally considered to be creatures of pure evil, and yet there is a romanticism about them too. They are eternally young and beautiful, never succumbing to aching joints, wrinkles and disease. They are usually wealthy, apparently having used their centuries of existence to accumulate vast riches we mortals can only dream of. They are seemingly above all laws, both of nature and of humankind. They are extremely seductive and bring death with a kiss. They are masters of magic and mind-control games. All of which adds up to one thing – a power that few can resist.

Most people drawn to magic will have come across the vampire legend at some point in their lives and may even have been slightly seduced by it! But to most magical people a vampire is more than a character in an old movie or a trendy TV series. He represents a total embrace of the darkness and acceptance of the innate predatory nature that lies deep within the human psyche. Although in movies and books the vampire is generally portrayed as totally evil, this is largely because most people, movie makers included, fear the darkness within themselves. Here I am going to try to show the vampire and the darkness in a new light, so to speak. And, no, this doesn't mean that we will be indulging in black magic.

Attuning with the vampire can help us to accept the darker side of nature and of ourselves. But let me clarify one thing here: there is a difference between accepting the darkness and giving yourself up to the dark side and the Left-hand Path, namely black magic. Accepting the darkness means that you can see the usefulness of winter, come to terms with the release of death and the promise of rebirth, and value the wisdom that is locked within nightmares. Giving yourself up to the dark side might involve dabbling in black magic or an unhealthy 'copy cat' interest in crime, and would probably lead to desperation and depression. I do not recommend you take this path!

Of all the lessons that the vampire has to teach us, perhaps the most important (if in a slightly distorted way) is that that death is not the end.

After this life, a new phase of existence awaits us. Just as the werewolf is a symbol of the battle between light and dark, so the vampire can be seen as a metaphor for the angel of death. In place of wings he has a swirling cloak; rather than an absolute demise, he offers the gift of a new life, free from earthly bonds and ties.

To release a soul

This spell will help to release a loved one, animal or human, who is on the point of death. It is not a way of playing God/ess; it is simply a little magic to help make the last struggle easier.

What you need
A black or white candle, matches or a lighter, a stick of Night Queen incense

What you do

✪ Light the candle and speak the following words:

> *If it is for the highest good of —— (state your loved one's name), let his/her soul return to the cosmos, and help me and mine to bear the loss.*

✪ Light the stick of Night Queen incense and say the following charm, visualising a peaceful end for your loved one as you speak:

> *Angel of Death, I light this spark*
> *To summon you here through the dark.*
> *Ease the pain and ease the flight;*
> *Take this soul on beams of light.*
> *By flame and smoke this plea I send;*
> *May magic and love bring a gentle end.*
> *Take this soul to a better place;*
> *Spirit fly, spirit race.*
> *Angel of Dark, Angel of Shadow,*
> *Bring release and ease the sorrow.*
> *So mote it be!*

  CREATURES OF THE NIGHT

✪ Allow the candle to burn down naturally. Remember that death is not the end and move forward into the light of your own life.

Hares

We end this chapter on a lighter note with the magical mad March hare. Although not a nocturnal animal as such, the hare prefers the hours of dusk and dawn to go about his business and is strongly associated with the moon. He is sacred to many gods and goddesses, among them Osiris, Eros, Cupid, Venus, Aphrodite, Hecate, Eostre and Diana. Unlike rabbits, who live in groups, hares are solitary animals and are quite territorial. This can lead to the 'boxing' matches for which they are famous! During the mating season, in early spring, the hare appears to go slightly mad, hence the well known expression 'as mad as a March hare'.

To the Celts the hare was a creature to be honoured and revered – to kill one meant that you would be struck with cowardice ever after. To the Anglo-Saxons the hare was the embodiment of the Corn Spirit. The white hare is thought to be the spirit of winter and is sacred to the White Goddess, or the Snow Queen as she is sometimes known.

Being linked to Diana, the moon goddess, the hare was associated with moon magic and witchcraft generally. In medieval times it was believed that witches would turn into hares to escape their inquisitors. The Scottish witch, Isobel Gowdie, claimed in her confession that she could shape-shift into the form of a hare. This is interesting, as Gowdie's confession was made without the use of torture and was apparently voluntary.

As a familiar, the hare can assist in all aspects of moon magic and can aid your powers of divination. It is said that the great warrior-queen Boudicca consulted a hare to discover the outcome of battles before she made war – a wise step that only a woman would think of! The hare can also teach us to live each day as it comes and to find true joy in our lives.

A spell for joy

What you need

A picture or statue of a hare, matches or a lighter

What you do

⭐ On the night of the full moon take the picture or statue of the hare to your altar. Light the illuminator candles and repeat the following spell nine times:

Magical hare,
Power we share.
Teach me to live without a care!

⭐ Blow out the candles and find joy in every day!

Healing Waters

Approximately two-thirds of the globe is covered in water, but, in spite of all our technology, the realms of the deep are still relatively alien to us. The ocean continues to guard many of her secrets jealously, and maybe, as humans, we will never fully understand aquatic creatures or the mysteries of the deep. But this doesn't mean that we cannot work with such creatures as familiars; indeed, in so doing we may develop a better understanding of them.

Magically speaking, the element of Water is associated with healing, emotions, dreams, intuition and psychic abilities. The spells in this chapter will focus on these areas.

A shrine to the sea

If you have an affinity with the ocean, you might like to create a shrine – or even a full working altar – dedicated to the sea. This would be an excellent place to honour aquatic power animals and to work spells that call on familiars such as fish, frogs and dolphins.

To make a sea shrine, cover your chosen surface with an altar cloth of blue or sea-green and place your illuminator candles in holders that have an aquatic theme. For instance, you might use candlesticks that are painted blue and bear images of fish and sea shells. If you have a little spare cash to invest in your magic, buy fancy candleholders fashioned to look like mermaids, sirens or sea horses.

Your shrine could include collections of sea shells and pebbles, and dried seaweed or starfish. It could also include pictures and statues or your chosen aquatic familiars. To represent divinity and magic include a statue of a goddess such as Aphrodite, or maybe the god Neptune. An oil burner that looks like a dolphin or a sea dragon is a nice addition. Above the shrine, hang pictures that depict the sea, and maybe also a sea horse wind-chime or a mermaid mobile. Over a period of time you can add to your shrine by investing in an appropriate water feature and collecting statues of mermaids, dolphins, fish, sea horses, starfish, sea birds, ships, lighthouses and so on.

If your shrine is also going to be a working altar, you might like to use a thin piece of driftwood as a wand and create a pentacle by drawing a five-pointed star on an upturned terracotta drainage pot and gluing tiny sea shells all along the lines you have drawn. Use sea-fragranced incense in your rituals, keeping sticks in a blue vase and cones in a sea shell trinket box. Remember to leave space on the altar for your magical spell-castings and keep it clean at all times.

Dolphins

We begin with what is perhaps the best-loved sea creature of all, the dolphin. I have always had a thing for dolphins. As a non-swimmer I am drawn to tales of dolphins saving people from drowning, and I am convinced that if a dolphin is near enough to help a swimmer in difficulty, he will go out of his way to save them. To me, dolphins are the knights of the sea, being chivalrous and protective, with a nature that carefully balances fierceness and gentleness.

In folklore the dolphin is known as the Arrow of the Sea and also the King of Fish, even though dolphins are actually mammals. It was once believed that dolphins swimming alongside a ship were an omen of good luck and foretold a safe journey. Leaping dolphins were indicative of an approaching sea storm, and sailors used to believe that dolphins governed the winds.

In mythology, dolphins are associated with Neptune, Dionysus, Apollo, Eros, Venus and Aphrodite. In some myths, mermaids ride dolphins across the waves, and Thetis, the Greek sea goddess, is sometimes depicted riding a sea shell chariot pulled by dolphins. Neptune has also been depicted this way, though more usually it is the white horses of the waves that draw his chariot.

As a familiar, the dolphin can teach us about having fun and indulging the playful side of our character. He can also help us to bring balance into our lives and is a very valuable power animal to call upon in working healing magic.

Healing ritual

To turn this ritual into a self-healing spell simply substitute for line five of the charm, 'Heal me now; make me well'.

What you need

A picture or a statue of a dolphin, some sea shells and/or pebbles, a stick of incense that carries the fragrance of a sea breeze or ocean surf, matches or a lighter, a CD of dolphin cries (optional)

What you do

✪ Take the representation of the dolphin to your altar and use the sea shells and/or pebbles to make a circle around it. Light the illuminator candles and the incense, and put on the CD if you are using one.

✪ Concentrate hard on the dolphin energy that you are calling on, and also on the person you wish to heal. Once you are relaxed and focused, begin to chant the following spell, continuing for as long as your focus remains strong:

King of Fish,
Grant my wish;
Hear now my plea:
Before the next tide does swell,
Heal the one I love so well.
So be it! Blessed be!

✪ Extinguish the candles, but leave all your tools in place for the next 24 hours.

Whales

Whales are the cousins of the dolphin but are considerably larger, ranging in size from 6 metres (20 feet) to 30 metres (100 feet) long. The blue whale is by far the biggest and holds the title for being the largest animal on the planet. Other species of whale include the sperm, the humpback, the grey, the bottlenose and, of course, the black and white orca, commonly known as the 'killer' whale.

Due to its size, sailors of old considered the whale to be a sea monster, and many myths evolved around it. One can only imagine how terrifying such a creature must have seemed to those with no knowledge about it! Tales were told of people being swallowed whole by a whale and then spat out later, apparently none the worse for their dreadful ordeal!

In parts of Scandinavia it was thought that whales had magical powers and would carry witches across the sea without harming them. It was also believed that witches could order whales to sink ships or cause shipwrecks.

In magical terms, whale familiars can be called upon to help us achieve balance, relax and accept a slower pace of life. In the past, whales were considered to be the keepers of all music, so you could adopt one as your familiar if you are, or wish to be, a musician.

For balance and relaxation

What you need
A candle scented with an oceanic fragrance, matches or a lighter, a CD of whale song

What you do
⭐ Light the candle and put the CD on to play. Then lie down in a comfortable position and begin to breath deeply. As you concentrate on your breathing and begin to relax, allow the whale song to connect you with this mighty familiar.

⭐ When you are ready, repeat the following charm silently in your head, keeping on chanting for about ten minutes:

> Mighty whale, balance my life;
> Guide me now away from strife.
> Bring your gifts of rest and calm;
> Help me to avoid all harm.

✪ When you have finished chanting, lie still and totally relaxed for a further 15 minutes. Try to do something quiet for the remainder of the day, so as not to upset your new-found sense of peace and calm.

Sea horses

Apart from being an incredibly beautiful creature, the sea horse can also be a useful ally as a power animal. It can teach us the gift of natural grace and beauty without vanity and can also give us the ability to go with the flow of life, rather than trying to fight against it. In mythology, sea horses were the steeds of the beautiful mermaids and sirens, linking them to seduction and sexuality.

To go with the flow

Figures of mermaids riding sea horses are widely available and can be bought quite cheaply, so buy one and use it for this spell if the idea appeals to you. You can chant this little spell in your head any time you feel that you are struggling against the tide of life.

What you need
A image or statue of a sea horse (optional)

What you do
✪ Focus on the representation of the sea horse if you are using one. Otherwise, bring the image of a sea horse to mind. Say the following charm three times:

> Aquatic equine, tiny sea horse,
> Let my problems run their course.
> Teach me all I need to know;
> Help me to go with the flow.

Seals and selkies

Seals are common visitors to and residents of our shores. The Romans believed that wearing a seal skin protected against lightning. In modern times the seal has become the victim of the vanity fur trade and its numbers have fallen dramatically as a result. Personally, I think that fur coats are beautiful, but only on the creatures that nature intended them for. If humans were meant to wear fur, we'd have been born with it on our backs!

Seals are widespread across the Highland coast and the islands of Scotland, and in Scottish folklore there are many tales of the seal people known as selkies. Selkies (pronounced silkies) are seals who can take on human shape and walk on land. They usually appear by moonlight in the guise of a beautiful maiden and, more unusually, of a handsome young man. They are very magical and are known to have the gift of healing.

To see a selkie is to fall head over heels in love! However, the only way to bind a selkie to the land is to steal and hide her seal skin, as without it she cannot return to the waves. The selkie will always be drawn to the sea nevertheless and, even if happily married with children, should she ever discover her pelt, she will immediately return to the ocean. A certain degree of discontent will always be felt by a selkie who is trapped on land.

Another tradition states that to keep a selkie in human form will bring fantastic luck while fishing and thus much wealth. This aspect of selkie lore was, for obvious reasons, particularly prevalent among fishermen and in fishing communities. The selkie tradition is so strong in Scotland that some clans claim seal people as their ancestors. The MacKays, for example, are known as 'the descendants of the seal'. Their story states that the old laird stole a seal woman's pelt and tricked her into marriage. However, the selkie eventually found her seal skin and returned to the sea, leaving behind her family and clan.

In most of the tales the selkie will eventually return to her true home. Thus in our magic the seal or selkie can help us through the pain of a separation or romantic break-up.

Selkie spell

If a love has ended, you can repeat this spell daily at dusk until the healing process is complete. This may take some considerable time. An ended love affair can take months, or even years, to get over, but making or accepting the break is always the hardest part. This spell will help you to heal yourself and move on with your life. If you live near the sea, spend as much time as you can on the beach and say the charm to the waves.

What you do

⭐ As dusk falls, go to your altar and focus on the image of a seal. When you see it clearly, call on the magical powers of the selkie in the following way:

> Selkie, my love and I must part;
> Please help me heal this broken heart.
> Give me strength to find my way,
> For with my love I cannot stay.
> Let new joy bubble like the ocean's foam,
> And let me find my true home.
> Selkie, selkie, heal my heart,
> For my love and I are worlds apart.

Fish

Fish come in all shapes, sizes and colours. They populate the world's oceans in their millions. In general, fish move around the waters in large groups, known as shoals. This is especially true of the smaller species, which are prey creatures. By swimming and moving together they make it extremely difficult for the predator to single out its lunch! Magically speaking, fish are sacred to Poseidon, Aphrodite, Neptune, Kuan Yin and Isis. They are symbols of fertility, love and abundance. The Celts believed that eating fish brought great wisdom, a belief that continues today in the idea that fish is 'brain food'. Within the Eastern tradition of feng shui it is believed that keeping goldfish will bring much wealth and prosperity into your life, and as a power animal the fish can help you to fill your life with abundance. A simple way to ensure that prosperity flows into your life is to keep two goldfish in a round bowl. Tend them well and they will magnetise riches, attracting new opportunities for you to increase your wealth. Or create a fish pond in your garden to the same effect.

For abundance and prosperity

What you need

A small piece of paper and some coloured pencils, patchouli essential oil

What you do

- ✪ Take the paper and crayons to your altar and draw a picture of a fish.
- ✪ Anoint the picture with patchouli oil (known for its money-drawing qualities).
- ✪ Finally, to protect your money and ensure that any you pay out returns to you threefold, draw a tiny fish, followed by 'x 3' in the bottom right-hand corner of all your notes and cheques.

Toads

We move now to a couple of freshwater animals. In the Middle Ages it was believed that toads were actually witches who had shape-shifted – and they are indeed sacred to Hecate, goddess of witches and the Underworld. As a creature that has been widely associated with magic and witchcraft, the toad has acquired an undeservedly bad reputation. It is in fact a gentle animal that divides its time between land and water. It is common throughout Britain, and is nocturnal, preferring to hibernate through the colder winter months.

As a familiar, the toad can assist with the development of witchcraft skills and psychic abilities.

To increase magical power

What you do

✪ Bring the image of a toad clearly to mind. Focusing on the image, chant the following words:

> *I call on the magic and wisdom of the toad, creature of Hecate, who links the elements of Water and Earth. I ask that you teach me and guide me through the ways of the witch. Sacred toad, I honour you and will work to develop your gift of psychic ability. I ask that you assist me in this endeavour. Blessed be!*

Frogs

Country folk often refer to the frog as the 'puddock'. Frogs spend more time in the water than on land and seem to be most at home in dark, shady ponds. The song of a frog is said to bring rain and thunder storms, while if one voluntarily wanders into your home, he is bringing you good luck. Frogs living in your garden means that you will never be without friends. It is considered very bad luck to harm, injure or kill a frog.

The frog, like the toad, is sacred to Hecate, and also to Isis, Aphrodite and Venus. To the ancient Egyptians the frog represented new life and rebirth, and even in the Christian belief system the frog is symbolic of resurrection. The frog is also a symbol of sexuality and lust, and has come to represent the loss of female virginity. The fairy tale *The Frog Prince*, which is actually the story of a young girl's awakening, illustrates this theme, with the frog symbolising initiation. Folklore states that should a girl come across a frog and kiss it, her true love will find his way to her soon. This is especially true if the frog is kissed on the summer solstice.

To find your prince

This spell is for all you romantic girls out there! If you believe that true love can be as good as a fairy tale but you've yet to find your handsome prince, then work a little magic on the night of the full moon.

What you need

2 red candles and suitable candleholders, matches or a lighter, your athame or an inscribing tool (a vegetable knife will do), rosemary essential oil, a small statue of a frog (these are available from garden centres), dried or fresh rose petals, rose perfume or essential oil, a slip of paper, a pen, a length of red thread, your cauldron or a fireproof dish

What you do

⭐ Go to your altar and light the illuminator candles. Inscribe the word 'Prince' on both red candles and anoint them with rosemary essential oil. Place them in their holders and light them.

⭐ Take the figure of the frog, kiss it and say:

> *Bring me my true prince.*

⭐ Place the frog between the red candles and surround all these items with an unbroken circle of rose petals.

⭐ Dab a little of the rose perfume or oil onto the frog's head and a little on to your pulse points – this serves to connect you and the spell.

⭐ Now spend some time thinking about the qualities and personality that you would like your prince to have. When you are clear about these, write them on the slip of paper. Roll the paper into a scroll and secure it with the red thread.

⭐ Light the scroll from one of the red candles and allow it to burn in your cauldron or the fireproof dish. Begin to chant the following spell, continuing for as long as you remain completely focused:

> *Bring together my prince and me*
> *That in his eyes true love I'll see.*
> *Happy ever after we will know;*
> *I kiss the frog this spell to sow.*
> *Bring together my prince and me*
> *That in his eyes true love I'll see.*

Come to me; I summon thee.
Do not hide; live by my side.
So mote it be!

⭐ Allow the red candles to burn down naturally to finish the spell (staying in the room for safety's sake while this happens). You can put out the illuminator candles if you wish. Repeat this spell every full moon until your prince makes himself known to you!

10

Feathered Friends

As creatures of air, birds rule over the magic of creativity and inspiration, so it is not surprising that we are enthralled by them. Throughout history, they have been regarded as mystical creatures and messengers from the gods. Their power of flight has alarmed us, puzzled us and urged us on to take to the skies. Without the example of birds there would be no planes, no helicopters, no leisurely gliders, no battle jets, no hang-gliding or paragliding and no space travel. In short, humankind would be firmly landlocked.

Birds are deeply ingrained in our language, figuring in expressions such as 'eats like a bird', 'winging it', 'flying high' and 'free as a bird'. Men sometimes refer to their female counterparts as 'birds', a term that stems in part from legends of sirens (see page 146) and of swan maidens, of which more later. The term was originally construed as flattering, though few women today would see it that way!

Birds have managed to retain much of their mystery and independence, and many superstitions have grown up around them. Some people believe that it is extremely unlucky to have any depiction of birds in the house, while others believe that certain types of bird, such as the robin, actually bring good luck. If a bird flies into the house, some see it as a bad omen, while others believe he is bringing good news from afar and are quick to thank him before he leaves. A bird tapping on a window with its beak is said to be a sign of death or a message that a newly departed loved one is close by. If you are on a journey, it is thought to be lucky to see a flock of geese travelling in the same direction as you, whereas if they are flying in the opposite direction your journey will be fraught with difficulty and delay.

In Greek mythology the god Zeus shape-shifted into a swan in order to magically seduce the beautiful Leda. The offspring of this union was

Helen of Troy. The Celts greatly esteemed all birds, and mystical Otherworldly birds often featured in their folklore. The three birds of Rhiannon, for example, were said to have the ability to awaken the dead with their song. The Irish goddess of beauty, Cliodhna, also kept singing birds; their gift was that of a healing song. The Celtic triple goddess, the Morrigan, could shape-shift into a raven. All members of the crow family, including the magpie, are sacred to her.

Moving on to the more fantastical members of the avian family, a malevolent bird of the Otherworld is the Scottish Boobrie, which haunts the lochs of Argyllshire, devouring sheep and goats as they graze. The Cockatrice is a dragon-like bird whose song can freeze the blood and bring about instant death – nice!

Swans

The swan is often considered to be the most beautiful bird on the planet. As a symbol of grace and purity, it is strongly linked to the Otherworld, and to see it gliding out of the mist is to understand something of its magic. Like most water-loving birds, it seems to float effortlessly across the water; there is little evidence of the strong and powerful movement going on beneath the surface. Swans mate for life and share a close bond with their family members.

Magically speaking, the swan is sacred to Zeus, Apollo, Merlin, Morgan le Fey, Aphrodite, Venus and the Valkyries. In folklore it is said to have the ability to invoke thunderstorms. In Scotland, to see three swans all flying together is said to be an omen of great disaster for the nation. A naturally quiet bird, the swan generally only hisses when annoyed and yet is believed to emit the most beautiful song just before it dies. This 'swan song' has been an inspiration to writers and musicians and has been a theme in many great plays and works of literature. Tradition states that to kill a swan is to invoke your own death, while to see a black swan is a sign of disaster and doom. Swans are also linked with ghosts and are said to lead spirits from the shadow world into our own world and back again. The Celts and Vikings believed that a swan boat would never sink and would ensure a safe arrival at one's destination. The Vikings sometimes used swan boats as funeral barges to ensure the safe arrival of their loved one in the afterlife.

FEATHERED FRIENDS

Swan maidens

There are several variations of the swan maiden legend. In Norse mythology, the Valkyries were said to shape-shift into swans. The Valkyries were battle maidens whose job was to take the souls of slain Viking warriors into the Norse Otherworld, Vallhalla.

This myth echoes the Celtic belief that swans are the guides of ghosts. In Celtic tradition, however, the swan maiden was a young girl who had been turned by magic into the form of a swan. Such a swan always wore a silver chain as a symbol of her enchantment, and in some tales whole groups of swans are bound together by these chains. However, it wasn't just the ladies who suffered this fate, for albeit that the stories of swan maidens are the best-known, occasionally princes and knights were treated to the same form of enchantment. Such a tale is that of the Children of Lir, in which Fionnuala and her three brothers are transformed into swans by their evil stepmother, who uses a druid staff to perform the magic.

The best-known version of the swan maiden legend is, of course, the ballet *Swan Lake*. Here, the beautiful Odette is turned into a swan by the evil magician Von Rothbart, and, despite winning the love of the handsome Prince Siegfried, in most productions she remains a swan maiden until her tragic end. In some versions of Swan Lake, however, Odette and Siegfried are ultimately united. This ending follows the scenario of some of the swan maiden myths, in which the maiden is released from the spell by the gift of true love. If a young man could see beyond the feathers to the maiden within and declare his love for her, then the enchantment was broken.

For beauty and grace

This spell uses the swan to enable us to acknowledge our beauty and learn to live with grace.

What you need
A small statue of a swan, an incense of your choice, matches or a lighter

What you do

⭐ Take the swan statue to your altar. Light the illuminator candles and the incense. Concentrate on the swan, using it as a focus to summon swan energies.

⭐ Once your focus is strong, repeat the following charm three times:

> *Grace and beauty bring to me;*
> *Shape and form it for all to see.*
> *Swan maiden, hear my plea;*
> *Let my looks enchanted be.*

Peacocks

The peacock (the female is called a peahen) is known for his striking appearance, fanning out his beautiful tail in an effort to impress potential mates or to intimidate enemies with his many 'eyes'. Peacocks are said to be vain and certainly do have a noticeable way of strutting around.

The peacock's call can be quite terrifying. Near to where I live is an aviary that houses a couple of peacocks. Occasionally I hear their call, and it never fails to make me shiver. During the day, especially throughout the long summer months, they can be quite noisy. The cry of the peacock is in complete opposition to its appearance. You would expect such a stunning bird to have a beautiful song – instead it shrieks out the sound of the Underworld! Hindus say that it has the voice of a devil or demon, and I am inclined to agree! But that is one of the wonderful things about these birds – they are just so Gothic!

In Persia the peacock once symbolised royalty, and it is undoubtedly a regal bird. It is sacred to Hera, Isis, Sarasvati and Lakshmi, and is considered by magical people to be a bird of paradise, which basically means that it is linked to the after-life and the Underworld/Otherworld. Peacocks are thought to bring luck both good and bad, and are said to perform their own version of a rain dance when the weather becomes too hot. In Britain it has long been a belief that to keep peacocks in the grounds will ward off intruders. Many great houses and stately homes still follow this practice. To bring peacock feathers into the house is thought to invite unhappiness and ill fortune, while to wear a single peacock feather is believed to avert the evil eye and negativity in general.

The peacock can teach us to become less shy and more self-confident. It is a great familiar to call upon when you want to be noticed or if you need to strut your stuff!

To increase confidence

What you do

⭐ Go to your altar and call to mind the image of a peacock. Maintaining this visualisation, summon his energies in the following way:

> *Feathered friend, royal bird,*
> *I summon now your gifts.*
> *Let my voice and mind be heard!*
> *My self-confidence now lifts.*
> *So mote it be!*

To warn of and protect against intruders

If you repeat this charm every month, preferably when the moon is full, the peacock image will be re-empowered and your home should remain safe from intruders. Remember to back up the spell in the mundane world with sensible security precautions.

What you need

A statue or picture of a peacock, or a peacock feather

What you do

⭐ Take your peacock representation and place it near your front door or the main entrance to your home. If you are using a feather, make sure you place it outside your house or flat.

⭐ Hold your hands over the image or feather, palms down, and empower it with the following words:

Graceful peacock of devil's cry,
Guard my home from those who pry.
I empower this image by this magical charm;
Should intruders call, raise the alarm!
So mote it be!

Doves

The dove is a symbol of peace, love and harmony. It is sacred to all love goddesses and moon goddesses, and in Christian tradition it is the symbol of Christ and the Holy Ghost. In China the dove represents long life, while to the ancient Celts it was a symbol of healing. In magic we can call on the dove's energies to bring the gift of love into our lives.

To call for love

What you need
5 pillar candles in white or a neutral shade, matches or a lighter, a trinket box with the image of doves on it or a pink envelope with the word 'dove' written on it, a sheet of paper, a pen

What you do

- ✪ Take your box or envelope to your altar and light the candles. Using the pillar candles, cast a circle, as described on page 29.
- ✪ On the sheet of paper write down all that you are looking for in a lover. Fold this paper up and place it in the trinket box or envelope.
- ✪ Now chant the following spell, continuing for as long as you remain focused:

    Bird of peace, beautiful dove,
    Bring to me the gift of love.

- ✪ When you have finished chanting, blow out the candles. Leave the trinket box on your altar until the spell manifests and your lover appears, then burn the spell paper and give thanks.

FEATHERED FRIENDS

Birds of the Morrigan

All members of the crow family are sacred to the Morrigan. Crows, ravens, blackbirds and magpies can all be called upon to help you attune with this Celtic goddess; however, be aware that she is not to be trifled with, for she is a dark goddess, linked strongly with the Otherworld. The simplest way to invoke her battle strength is to call on her protective qualities by wearing a raven charm. However, each of her birds has its own magical attributes.

Ravens

These large, high-flying birds feed on carrion, but they will also hunt small mammals. They are strongly associated with powers of guardianship, as is illustrated by the legend of the Tower of London. It is said that if the ravens living there ever leave, England will fall and disaster will strike the monarchy. It is the job of the Beefeaters to take care of the ravens and see that they remain at the Tower, thus guarding against the dreadful prophecy. I think we are supposed to overlook the fact that the birds are caged and their wings clipped – personally I'd find it easier to drop my jaw and assume the correct expression if the birds were given a choice in the matter! As things stand I feel that they are being exploited as a tourist attraction.

To call on the energies of a raven for his guardianship, wear a raven charm or meditate on a picture of a raven.

Crows

Crows are messengers from the Otherworld. If one nests in your garden, it is a sign that benevolent spirits are nearby, while one sitting on the roof of your house indicates that you are protected by the Morrigan.

Spell for power and enchantment

Whenever you see a crow in your garden, call out this spell to increase your magical power:

Bird of the Morrigan, bestow on me your Queen's gifts of magic and enchantment. Give me great power that I may use it wisely. Protect me and guard my home with the strength of the Morrigan. So mote it be! Blessed be!

Magpies

Magpies are birds of augury: you can divine aspects of your future by counting how many birds there are together in a group. Many rhymes spell out the key to this form of divination; the following is the one I was taught as a child – if you are more comfortable with a different version, then by all means go with that.

One for sorrow, two for joy,
Three for a girl, four for a boy,
Five for silver, six for gold,
Seven for a secret never to be told.
Eight together brings a kiss,
Nine together – make a wish.

The fact that the poem ends at nine, the number of the triple goddess, illustrates the magpie's strong link with the Morrigan and with witchcraft in general.

Robins

Known in Britain as the herald of winter, the robin redbreast is a favourite with almost everyone. It is said that you should make a wish on the first robin you see each winter, and if you make your wish before the winter solstice, it is sure to come true. In magical terms, the robin is the bird of Yuletide, a fire festival, and of all fire rituals and spells.

In England the robin is the bird of Robin Hood, and to see one in a forest is a sign of good fortune. According to folklore, the robin brought the fire of the sun to mankind and that is how he burnt his breast. In Wales it is said that to kill a robin will invoke a house fire in which the culprit will lose everything. There is also an old superstition that to see a robin with an injured wing means that you will break your arm.

As a weather omen, a robin hidden in a hedge indicates a heavy rainfall, while one sitting out in the open is a sign that a stretch of good weather is on the way. If he repeatedly ruffles up his feathers, however, it is a sign of heavy snow to come and possibly a blizzard. In Norse mythology the robin is sacred to Thor and is said to have the power to bring on a snowstorm.

To bring luck for a year

This is a spell for the winter solstice, or Yuletide, 21st December. If you celebrate Christmas, you might like to perform it on Christmas Eve instead.

What you need
Matches or a lighter; a stick of Yuletide incense, such as pine, holly or cinnamon; a small model robin – the type sold for Christmas cakes or Christmas trees will do; 1 red and 1 green candle and appropriate candleholders

What you do
✪ Take all the items to your altar and light the illuminator candles. Light the incense and place the robin in the centre of the altar, with the red candle on the right and the green candle on the left. Light both candles.

✪ Chant the following spell:

> *Robin redbreast, hear this plea:*
> *Bring fortune and good luck to me.*
> *Little bird of bright good cheer,*
> *Bring me luck through the coming year.*
> *Bird of thunder, bird of Thor,*
> *Bring good fortune to my door.*
> *Bird of Yuletide, bird of fire,*
> *Help me attain all I desire.*
> *I send the spell and let it go;*
> *As I will, it shall be so!*

⭐ Allow the candles to burn for as long as you are in the room, putting them out safely before you go about your Yuletide celebrations or Christmas preparations.

Animal Miscellany

I n this chapter we will be exploring the magical associations of those animals that don't fit neatly into other categories. We will begin with a creature that has a long historical – and, indeed, prehistorical – connection with magic and witchcraft ...

Snakes

Only in the Judaeo-Christian tradition are snakes thought of as evil; in other religions of the world they are honoured and revered. The snake is held sacred to many gods and goddesses, among them Zeus, Apollo, Boreas, Cuchulain, Fionn, Conall, Demeter, Isis, Bast, Medusa, Gaia, Astarte, Nimue and Vivienne.

Prior to the evolution of Christianity, the snake was the symbol of the Great Mother Goddess. It has been linked with fertility and healing, death and the Otherworld, sexuality and sensuality. It is a creature of magic and mystery that has the ability to fill people with fear and panic. It is a popular familiar among witches, and many keep snakes as pets and companions.

I love snakes, and at a party quite recently I was lucky enough to have the chance to handle two or three. My favourite was a beautiful terracotta colour, and she coiled herself around my wrist like a living bracelet! Contrary to popular belief, snakes are not slimy or wet. They are dry and have a satin-like feel to them that is actually very pleasant. One of the snakes was surprisingly swift and extremely agile – I adored her completely! I also discovered that snakes like nothing better than to be tickled under the chin and will stretch out their necks in much the same way as a cat! They even seem to smile! This image doesn't quite fit with their reputation for being the world's greatest evil!

None of our native snakes in Britain is poisonous. However, some foreign species carry a deadly venom, so where exotic pets and foreign holidays are concerned it's probably better not to touch them unless you know one snake from the other or are with someone who does.

As creatures who shed their skin, snakes have come to represent rebirth and reincarnation. Thus they are symbolic of immortality and of the fifth element, which is known as Spirit or Akasha. Snakes also feature in the caduceus, a magical staff and a symbol of great magical authority, around which two snakes intertwine their heads at the top, facing in opposite directions. The caduceus was carried by the god Hermes, by magicians and alchemists such as Merlin, and by those with the ability to heal. Today the sign of the caduceus is the symbol of the medical profession.

The ouroborus, a snake swallowing its own tail, is a symbol of eternity. Jewellery fashioned into this shape was often exchanged between lovers during the early Middle Ages as a sign of eternal love. A ring formed into a snake is said to bring long life and good health to the one who wears it.

In Greek mythology the personification of the north wind was known as Boreas. He was said to have a tail like a serpent. He could also bring along with him a terrific thunderstorm, so lightning was known as 'the sky serpent'.

Certain areas of Britain are closely connected to snake mythology. The River Wharf in Yorkshire, for instance, is said to be inhabited and guarded by a snake goddess called Verbeia. In Pembrokeshire there is a well reputed to contain a priceless golden torc – and a guardian snake that bites any would-be thief! Further north, in Aberdeenshire, the Maiden's Well is said to be the home of a winged serpent. All these tales illustrate another aspect of serpent folklore: the snake's strong association with the element of water and with sacred wells, another symbol of the Goddess.

As a familiar, the snake is strongly associated with guardianship. A small wood carving of a snake could be placed where you keep your magical tools, to guard and protect them. Alternatively, you could keep your tools in a chest decorated with a snake design. A figure of a snake by your front door will protect your home, and snake jewellery will keep you from harm. Serpents are also linked with prophecy and divination, so you could keep your favourite set of tarot cards in a box engraved with serpents, or you could embroider snakes onto a velvet tarot pouch. If your needlepoint skills are limited, you can use a canvas pouch and fabric paints to the same effect.

In occult shops it is possible to buy books of shadows with metal snake-like hinges and a serpent design on the cover. If snake energy appeals to you, you might like to invest in one of these – but be warned, they can be quite pricey! If you plan to work with snakes as your main familiar, then keep your eyes peeled for a caduceus staff, sometimes available from Wiccan and new age stores. This will also be useful if you plan to work a lot of dragon magic – indeed, dragons and serpents are related in a magical sense. If finances are a problem, then take a look in your local ethnic store, where you will probably find bags, pouches, boxes and incense holders in beautiful jewel colours and sparkling with sequins in snake designs. Such items can all be used magically and need not break the bank!

As the snake grows, it sheds its skin and is reborn more beautiful and colourful than before. We can therefore call on snake energy whenever we feel we need to alter our personal appearance or change our image.

The serpent's egg

The serpent's egg was an amulet worn by chief druids. It is sometimes called 'the snake stone' or 'the druid's glass'. Whether these eggs were actual magical tools or simply the invention of fable is not clear; however, it was believed that such an amulet could protect against all magic and enchantments, and even bestow omnipotence upon its wearer, giving complete control over the serpent world. Could this be the inspiration behind J K Rowling's notion of 'serpent tongue'? Needless to say, serpents' eggs were much sought after.

To shed an old skin

We've all heard the phrase, 'Never judge a book by its cover', and yet that is exactly what we do. We take people in at a glance and judge them by their appearance. Take that into consideration when you are dressing each morning. Of course we've all got clothes we relax around the house in, but if you wouldn't want your dream man/woman to see you in them, then don't leave the house without changing first!

Clothes are almost a magical tool in themselves! With a quick change we can alter our persona and become someone else in an instant. The clothes in my wardrobe (and there are many!) help me to express various facets of my character and portray different images of myself to the outside world. Images such as biker chick, girl next door, Gothic witch, sexy witch, medieval maiden, eternal romantic, equestrienne and so on all enable me to portray the different aspects of who I am.

Take a good long look at yourself and your whole wardrobe – including nightwear and lingerie. What do your clothes say about you? Is this the image you want to portray? Is it really you? Are you making the most of your assets or selling yourself short? Does your wardrobe show what an exciting, multifaceted person you are or do you find yourself wearing the same sort of thing day in and day out? If you are dissatisfied with your image, snake energy can help.

Before working this spell, have a good clear-out and give any clothes you no longer want or wear to charity. (This will make room for lots of new goodies too. You see, feminine logic never takes a day off!)

What you do

☆ Stand before your mirror skyclad (naked) and say the following spell three times:

> *As snakes coil and turn,*
> *My old image I burn.*
> *Shedding my skin to be free,*
> *I would have people know*
> *That I'm more than I show,*
> *As I grow and become a new me!*

☆ Now keep an eye out for any bargains that suit your new image, and treat yourself.

Elephants

Elephants are the largest creatures on land and probably the most powerful too. They can weigh up to four tons and live for as long as 80 years. There are two species of elephant, the Indian and the African, and the easiest way to tell them apart is to count the nails on the hind feet. The Indian elephant has four or five, while the African only has three.

Both Indian and African elephants are now endangered species, having been cruelly hunted for ivory. The ivory trade is illegal and, like the fur trade, is a totally despicable practice.

Elephants are gentle creatures, living together in family groups and even performing rituals! They show tremendous joy at the birth of a new baby and will spin round and round in circles in a dance of welcome. They also go into mourning for a lost member of the herd, even revisiting the 'graveside' and lovingly fondling the bones with their trunks. They are the only members of the animal kingdom who indulge in such rites – other than ourselves of course.

The lucky white elephant is sometimes found among the Indian species. It is thought to bring good fortune and is held particularly sacred, so it is generally presented as a gift to a local temple. The elephant-headed Hindu god Ganesha is said to be the remover of obstacles and is very popular among Hindus. In Hinduism the elephant is symbolic of royalty, wisdom, intelligence and long life.

Elephant energy can help to remove any blocks in your life and give you the energy to move forwards.

To remove obstacles and increase strength

What you need
Matches or a lighter, a small figure of Ganesha, 5 tea-lights and appropriate holders, 5 pillar candles in white or a neutral shade

What you do
✪ Go to your altar and light the illuminator candles. Place the statue of Ganesha in the middle of the altar and surround him with a circle of five (unlighted) tea-lights.

- ✪ Using the pillar candles and following the instructions on page 29, cast the main Circle around yourself.
- ✪ Light the tea-lights and say the following spell three times:

> *The Circle within the Circle*
> *Holds the force that is Ganesha,*
> *Remover of obstacles,*
> *Bringer of elephant strength.*
> *I summon your gifts*
> *Across time and space;*
> *I summon your gifts*
> *Within sacred space.*
> *So mote it be!*

Bees

In ancient Egypt, bees were considered to be the tears of the sun god Ra. They represent birth, death and rebirth, and have been considered sacred by many ancient cultures. In ancient Greece it was thought that good souls came back to earth in the form of bees, and golden honey is the symbol of Aphrodite the goddess of love and beauty. As creatures of the Goddess, bees were linked to the moon, and Demeter, the corn goddess was also known as the Queen Bee.

Bees are said to predict a death in a family by flying around the house three times. If a bee actually flies into your home, it is bringing blessings and good fortune, so thank it before it leaves. A bee that flies around a sleeping baby is bestowing the gift of a long and happy life and should never be shooed away. It is very unlucky to kill a bee, as these creatures are the messengers of the gods. To keep an image of a bee in the kitchen will ensure plentiful food and general abundance, while certain bedroom activities can be encouraged by placing a honey pot under the bed! On that note, ancient tradition states that a virgin cannot be stung by a bee.

Anyone who keeps bees should always make sure they are up to date on the gossip – tradition has it that your bees should be told of family births, deaths and wedding plans.

Bee energy can be called upon to help us become the centre of attention – in a positive way.

Queen bee spell

We all like to be at the centre of things sometimes, with everyone revolving around us. It's good to be the hub of the universe once in a while! Cast this spell if you feel you could use this type of attention. But be aware that if you abuse this spell by casting it too often, you may end up getting stung!

What you need
A picture of a bee (optional)

What you do

✪ Concentrate hard on the bee image or visualise a bee in your mind's eye. Once you can see the image clearly, chant the following words:

> *Honey, honey, come to me;*
> *I am the Queen – the Queen Bee.*
> *Everyone revolves around me,*
> *For I am the Queen – the Queen Bee!*

Bears

It seems almost impossible that bears once roamed the British countryside, yet they only died out in this country during the Middle Ages, largely due to hunting and the practice of bear baiting. At one time, brown bears were numerous throughout England, Scotland and Wales.

In mythology the bear is associated with the goddesses Artemis and Atalanta, and the Gaulish bear goddess Arduinna. It was held to be a sacred creature by the Celts, who wore bearskins to summon strength during battle. Ancient castles were furnished with bear pelts, and figures of bear have been found as grave gifts in ancient Celtic burial sites. Perhaps the bear's most famous association, though, is King Arthur. Arthur, meaning 'great bear', was a powerful warrior king.

Tales of him, his valiant knights of the Round Table and his kingdom of Camelot are still often told today. His legend will never die, and he is a popular deity among those modern witches who lean towards the Celtic tradition.

Bear cults are a part of the folkloric history of many countries, including Britain, Norway, Finland and Lapland. And, of course, the Native Americans hold the bear sacred too. It is thought that the bear may hold the title of 'most sacred animal the world over'! Incidentally, the phrase 'licking into shape' comes from the folk belief that bear cubs are born unformed and the mother bear has to lick them into the correct shape!

As a familiar, the bear can teach us the wisdom of our ancient ancestors, and as a spirit guide it can lead us to our true path in life and help us to make important decisions.

For ancestral wisdom

What you need
5 pillar candles in white or a neutral colour, matches or a lighter, a packet of incense of your chosen fragrance

What you do
- Using the pillar candles and following the instructions on page 29, cast a Circle. The Spirit Bear travels via smoke, so light plenty of incense.
- When the air is nice and smoky, visualise a brown bear standing tall upon his hind legs and call his energies to you using the following words:

  Great Spirit Bear, I summon you. Guide me to my true path and help me to share in the wisdom of my ancestors. Through time and space I honour you, and I ask that you guide me and surround me with your strength and wisdom. So mote it be! Blessed be!

- Stay within the circle until the incense has burnt down and the smoke has faded. Then take down the Circle and go about your day.

Familiar Fantasy

We now move completely into the astral realm and focus on familiars of a mythical origin. These creatures are also known as elementals and, although they can be quite elusive at first, once you have begun to work with them as familiars, you will discover that they are true allies and are strong and powerful in their own right.

Although mythical creatures do not exist in our world, we can still bring them into our life by attuning with them and working with them magically. One way to do this is by filling your home with pictures and statues of the magical beasts you would like to work with. For example, I love mermaid energy, and my bedroom is full of mermaid images, including fine art pictures, figurines, a wooden wall plaque carved into the shape of a swimming mermaid, a ceramic wall plaque holding an oyster shell and pearl, a bronze water feature and even an altar table fashioned to look like a relaxing mermaid. I also love unicorns and winged horses, and have a collection of figures to bring these magical energies into my home too. In my lounge I have dragons, and I am currently working on finding statues of satyrs and centaurs.

As you read this, you may already know which mythical creature has filtered into your life, and you may have pictures of dragons, unicorns, sirens or whatever throughout your home. Or you may have loved a particular creature since childhood – the phoenix perhaps, or the griffin. The fact is that most people drawn to magic have an affinity with at least one species of mythical beast. In this chapter we will be looking at how to develop that affinity into a working magical relationship, calling on your favourite fantasy creature as a familiar and magical companion.

The phoenix

A couple of years ago I had a letter from a reader who was experiencing great troubles in her life. She had only recently discovered magic and witchcraft, my book being one of the first she had read on the subject, and she wrote to thank me for writing the book and to tell me her new magical name – Phoenix.

This is a popular name with newcomers, as it signifies entry into a new life, but it struck me at the time that such a name was perfect for someone who was going through a tough time and was using magic to improve her life. I guess her familiar really was making contact and was hoping to teach her that she could rise from the flames of her troubles and move on into a new and better way of being. This is, after all, the main lesson of the phoenix.

The phoenix is probably the most beautiful bird of mythology. Said to be larger than a golden eagle, but with elongated tail feathers similar to those of a pheasant or a peacock, the phoenix has a shimmering plumage of deep red, amber and gold, echoing the flames and embers of a glowing fire. It sacrifices itself by bursting into flames and then rises again, reborn from the ashes more beautiful than ever. Thus the phoenix is symbolic of resurrection and is sacred to gods such as Osiris and Ra, and, some hold, to Jesus. The phoenix is also associated with Circe, the goddess of enchantment.

Traditionally, the phoenix lives for 500 years before it returns to the fire, and its tears are said to have the power to heal any wound or disease. If a phoenix appears to you in your dreams, it is a sign that a great beneficial change will occur in your life, that some aspect of you will be reborn and that there will be a new beginning of some kind.

The phoenix is a bird of the sun and, due to its association with the element of Fire, it can help us to become more passionate about life in general or within a relationship. The phoenix can also assist us to rise above our troubles and be reborn into a more carefree phase of life.

To rise from the flames

What you need
A statue or picture of a phoenix – though these are difficult to come by, so you will probably have to visualise the phoenix in your mind's eye

What you do
- ⭐ Concentrate on the representation of the phoenix or clearly visualise one, perched before you in a shimmer of red and gold feathers. Tell the phoenix your troubles, plainly stating the challenges you face.
- ⭐ Speak the following charm below five times (one for each century of the bird's lifetime):

  Magical bird, born of fire,
  Take my troubles into the flame;
  Phoenix, hear now my desire;
  Help me rise up and begin again.

To increase passion

You can use this spell to increase passion in your life in general or in a relationship.

What you do
- ⭐ Bring to your mind's eye the image of a phoenix. When you have a clear picture of the phoenix, repeat the following chant for as long as you can maintain focus:

  Magical phoenix, born of fire,
  Fill my life with passion and desire.

Mermaids and sirens

As with vampires, I am really stretching a point here, but I find these part-human/part-animal creatures so fascinating that I wanted to give them a brief mention in this book.

Mermaids and sirens are the elementals of water. Sometimes they are collectively known as undines, and they are strongly associated with feminine charms and beauty. Traditionally, they have long, flowing tresses and are irresistible to men. They are the witches of the deep. Their song is said to lure unwary sailors to their death, although these magical creatures also have a more benevolent side.

Mermaids and sirens differ slightly from one another in appearance. The mermaid is of female form to her waist, and her lower half is that of a fish, with beautiful iridescent scales and a tail that fans out gracefully where her feet would otherwise be. The siren has the body of a woman from top to bottom. She also has the ability to shape-shift into a large bird. Magically speaking, the siren links the two realms of water and air, while the mermaid is the guardian of the oceans and all large bodies of water.

Attuning with mermaids and sirens can help you to discover your own inner beauty and powers of attraction. They are often the spirit guides of girls and women, for whom they are powerful protectors, and they can also be called upon to guard you or your daughter, sister and so on, or to protect you from unwanted advances. As a familiar they can assist in magical enchantments, love spells, creativity, inspiration and even singing lessons! To bring more love into your life, fill your home with mermaid energy by decorating it with mermaid pictures, statues and so on. But by far the most powerful spell a mermaid or siren can help you with is a seduction spell! For more, read on ...

Siren song

What you need
An image of a mermaid or siren, a CD of ocean sounds (optional), matches or a lighter, incense of a marine fragrance, 5 pillar candles in white or a neutral colour, a photo of your love (if you are in a relationship)

What you do
- ⚝ Take everything to your altar and light the illuminator candles. Put on the CD if you are using one, and light the illuminator candles and incense. If you are using a photo, place it, together with the mermaid image, on the altar.
- ⚝ Using the pillar candles and following the instructions on page 29, cast the Circle.
- ⚝ Concentrating on the figure of the mermaid or siren, invoke siren energy using the following words:

> *Beautiful siren, enchantress and seductress, I ask that you bestow your gifts upon me that I may attract love and passion into my life. Be with me and assist me in my magical working.*

- ⚝ Now concentrate on the photo of your love or, if you are not in a relationship, on the qualities of your ideal partner and on bringing him to you. Feel the siren's energies around you and imagine that you are absorbing them into yourself. You are becoming a siren! When you feel ready, chant the following siren song for as long as you can remain focused:

> *Come to me, I summon thee;*
> *Hear now my siren song.*
> *Come to me, I summon thee,*
> *For I have loved thee long.*
> *Swim with me, spin with me,*
> *Live with me and be my love.*
> *Play with me, lay with me;*
> *I'll take you to the stars above.*

Dance with me, entranced you'll be;
I cast my witch's web out wide.
Think of me, dream of me;
From my charms you cannot hide!
Look for me, feel for me;
The magic of my spell unfurls.
Teach me and reach out for me;
My love for you will rock your world.
Let me lead you by the hand
To my secret place.
Your will succumbs to my demand,
Crossing time and space.
See my lips, my swaying hips;
Your gaze is locked with mine.
Feel my power, 'tis the hour;
Come now – you are mine!

⭐ Blow out all the candles and allow the spell to play itself out in your life. Repeat as desired!

Unicorns

The unicorn, king of all equines, is found in folklore throughout the world. It is most usually depicted as a pure white horse with a long spiral horn projecting from its forehead. However, in some cultures it is more stag- than horse-like, while in other parts of the world it has the appearance of a goat, and it may be grey, black, blue, roan or dappled in colour.

Some of you, I'm sure, will have had an affinity with the unicorn since you were very young. Many children are drawn to the unicorn and believe fully in its existence in our world. I can remember as a small child being told that the unicorn had missed Noah's Ark and that was why it could be seen only in dreams and fairy tales. A nice story, and it made me happy to think that the unicorn had once lived in our world and was still somehow connected to it. The unicorn is a symbol of purity and innocence, and is thus associated with young children.

Unicorns are also connected with magic, enchantment, the faerie realm, speed, beauty, chastity, valour and ferocity when needed. Legend states that a unicorn gallops so swiftly it can never be captured. Instead it has to be lured into a trap baited with a fair maiden (a virgin). The unicorn cannot resist the attraction of innocence and will always fall into the trap.

Unicorns were said to live in forests or groves of apple trees. The apple is, of course, a symbol of Avalon, the Celtic Otherworld, and this association illustrates the unicorn's ability to move between the worlds. He is a guardian of treasures kept in a chest made of cedarwood, and he is also believed to hold the secrets of true alchemy. The use of apple or cedarwood essential oil in ritual can help you to connect with this beautiful creature.

Although unicorns are not considered to have a physical existence on the material plane, there have nevertheless been occasional sightings of them. It is not clear what prompts them to make such a visitation, and it is not known how widespread such sightings are. Unlike UFO sightings, which have achieved some degree of credibility in the last few years, encounters with a unicorn are generally considered to be impossible, and so such accounts are usually kept under wraps. The Wiccan author Yasmine Galenorn has been brave enough to describe her own meeting in one of her books, *Embracing the*

Moon, and it makes for interesting reading. This is the kind of thing that happens when you begin to live a magical life – doors you never knew existed will open! A friend of mine is also convinced that she saw a unicorn in her back garden and has given me permission to recount her tale here. I hope that you will read the following with an open and magical mind ...

My friend Beth was going through a really tough time, having just ended a long-term relationship with her fiancé. Although she was still deeply in love with this man, and he with her, she had broken off the engagement because she knew that she could no longer live with his attitude to certain things. In the weeks and months that followed, Beth was very low and felt that she had no direction in her life. She was drifting through each day, constantly questioning her decision and wondering where her life was going.

Her visitation began as a dream. In it she was standing by her bedroom window, looking out over the moon-lit garden, and there, at the far end of the lawn beneath the fir trees, stood a pure white unicorn. Beth knew that she had to go to the creature, so she went downstairs, unlocked the back door and went out into her garden. The unicorn turned to look at her as she walked down the garden path, and somehow Beth knew that she must go no further.

She stood gazing at the beautiful unicorn before her for some time, and the unicorn gazed right back! Then, slowly, consciousness returned and Beth woke up – to find herself standing in her garden, in her nightie, staring at a unicorn, who remained for half a second and then vanished!

Puzzled and confused as to what had actually happened, Beth went back into the house and made herself a cup of tea. As she reflected on what she had seen, she began to find a new hope and happiness in her heart. A couple of days later she saw a figure of a unicorn in a shop window, so she went in and bought

FAMILIAR FANTASY

it, and now it sits proudly on her altar as a reminder of her special visitor.

It was shortly after this magical evening that Beth made a vow of chastity to herself, swearing to remain without sex until she found true love again. When I spoke to her about her experience she told me:

'Seeing the unicorn made me realise that it was the man, not the love that let me down. I'm happy to be single until true love comes my way again. Besides, it gives me more time for my magic!'

Beth is still convinced that her visitation was a gift to help her understand her heart and move on with her life.

While the above tale may be hard for the average Joe (or Jane) Doe to swallow, magical people may find it much easier to accept as truth. Certainly, Beth's vow of chastity was consistent with the presence of unicorn energy. These beautiful creatures have much to teach us if we open our hearts and minds and let them in.

The allicorn

'Allicorn' is the name given to the spiralling horn on the unicorn's head. It is blessed with magical properties, and at one time it was believed that the unicorn had been hunted to extinction for the gift of its horn. During the Middle Ages many fake allicorns were in circulation and were widely accepted as genuine. They were used as magical wands by would-be alchemists and were also fashioned into drinking horns, as the main attribute of the allicorn was that it could detect all poisons and purify them, rendering them quite harmless. Allicorns were also said to be able to purify water. It was believed that a unicorn would dip its horn into a lake or stream before drinking from it.

Imitation allicorns, made of glass, crystal, silver or pewter, are still available to buy as an unusual ornament, although they can be quite difficult to find and can be expensive. If the idea of having one appeals to you, then ask the unicorn to help you find one. An imitation allicorn would make a great magical wand. Keep a look out in gift shops and on junk stalls. You may be lucky.

To call for an allicorn

What you need
A figure or picture of a unicorn, a tea-light and an appropriate holder, matches or a lighter, cedarwood essential oil, a stick of cedarwood incense (optional)

What you do

⭐ Take everything to your altar. Light the illuminator candles and the incense if you are using it. Place the unicorn in the centre of the altar, with the tea-light, in its holder, just in front. Add two drops of the cedarwood oil to the surface of the tea-light and light the wick.

⭐ Sit comfortably and place your hands, palms up, on either side of the tea-light. Open your palms as if receiving what you are about to call for. Now call for your allicorn by chanting the following charm, continuing for as long as your focus remains strong:

> *Unicorn, unicorn,*
> *Bring to me an allicorn!*

⭐ Allow the tea-light to burn down naturally. Keep your eyes peeled for your allicorn. You will generally find that it will come to you when you are in a position to afford it, maybe after a birthday or a tax rebate, for example. Cast this spell regularly until your allicorn has found its way to you.

Spell for purity

Unicorns can bestow upon us purity of heart and mind. If you feel a little jaded by the modern world and would like to bring some old-fashioned purity into your life, try this spell.

What you need
A figure or picture of a unicorn

What you do
✪ Meditate upon the image of the unicorn. Chant the following magical poem and allow it to help in your visualisation:

> Here he comes, the mightiest of steeds,
> Thinking good thoughts, doing good deeds.
> See him now, so wholesome and pure,
> Captured only by the virgin's lure.
> See the small beard, curly and soft;
> See how he holds his proud head aloft,
> Loyal and fierce, brave and true,
> Bold and courageous yet gentle too.
> His long silver tail like a waterfall,
> Shaking his mane, he utters a call.
> Find him only in the magical grove,
> The creature that teaches all to love.
> Be not afraid, he will do you no harm,
> Unless he is hunted for his wondrous charm.
> See how he moves with beauty and grace;
> See the wisdom in his noble face.
> Prince of all horses, friend to all,
> And there on his head, standing tall,
> Is his downfall and his pride,
> The reason that he needs to hide,
> The glittering, magical, spiralled horn,
> For he is the magnificent unicorn.
> I call his presence here to me
> To fill my heart with purity.
> So mote it be!

To see a unicorn

Like many astral creatures, the unicorn can be quite shy, so do your best to attune with its energy before you call it. You could do this by beginning to collect statues and pictures of unicorns. If you are an artist, you could make your own unicorn artwork. Alternatively, work with the unicorn in your meditations. Once you feel that you have made a psychic link with the unicorn, perform this spell.

What you need
A picture or object to represent the unicorn realm, 5 pillar candles in white or a neutral shade, matches or a lighter

What you do

⭐ Take everything to the altar and light the illuminator candles. Using the pillar candles and following the instructions on page 29, cast a Circle.

⭐ Focusing on the unicorn picture or object, bring to mind the image of a unicorn. When you have the image clear, call out the following invitation (or one of your own choosing):

> *I send these words through time and space*
> *To bring a unicorn to this place.*
> *Be it today, or be it soon,*
> *Be it by the light of the magical moon,*
> *Be it in flesh or be it in dreams,*
> *The beautiful unicorn will be seen*
> *By I who walk the witch's road.*
> *Unicorn strength now lightens my load.*
> *Unicorn come to me,*
> *Your beauty I would wish to see.*
> *Unicorn come to me!*
> *This is my will. So mote it be!*

⭐ Close your Circle. In the weeks that follow, make careful note of your dreams. This may be where the unicorn makes its appearance.

Winged horses

The winged horse is another very beautiful mythical beast. The most famous winged horse of all is, of course, Pegasus, the beautiful white horse with huge angelic wings in Greek mythology. Winged horses are also known as 'moon steeds' as they are linked to the moon and the Goddess. Some winged horses also have an allicorn, making them doubly powerful.

Seeing a winged horse in your dreams is sometimes an indication of needing to escape temporarily from a situation in your life. Such a dream could be a sign that you should take a holiday or a break from work, or just schedule in some 'me' time. Winged horses always bring us back to where they found us; nevertheless, a little trip with one is always beneficial.

As a familiar, the winged horse can help us to ascend to new heights, soar above problems and rise to all challenges. He can assist us in learning the arts of meditation or astral travel. He is the guardian animal of true poets and poetic inspiration, and can even be called upon to bring us fame and fortune.

In the following exercise, we call upon Pegasus to take us on an astral journey ...

Pegasus meditation

Calling on Pegasus as a companion in meditation is an excellent way to build your confidence in this area of magic. Pegasus is a gentle steed; he will take care of you and instil in you a feeling of safety and security. Like all the meditations and journeys in this book, the Pegasus Meditation is perfectly safe; however, feelings of fear and panic are occasionally experienced by those who are new to the concept of meditation and astral journeying. Working with Pegasus will help you to feel confident and comfortable while you are in a meditative state.

For this exercise, you can record the meditation on an audiotape or ask a friend to read it to you. Either way, make sure there are plenty of pauses between sentences so that you have time to visualise fully.

What you need
Candles of your choice, some incense, matches or a lighter, a CD of

new age or classical music (optional), some comfortable cushions

What you do

- ✪ Find a quiet space where you will not be disturbed. Prepare the area by locking the door, turning off the ringer on the phone, and lighting the incense and candles. If you are using a CD, turn it on to play softly in the background. Place the cushions on the floor and then settle yourself down in a comfortable position – but make sure that your spine is straight.

- ✪ Concentrate on your breathing and feel yourself beginning to relax. Try not to think of mundane matters, as this is your magical time. Once you feel fully relaxed, turn on the tape or ask your friend to start reading the following meditation:

> *A shimmering, silver-white light surrounds you. It is bright but not blinding, and it does not hurt your eyes. As the light fills the room, you hear the soft whicker of a horse. Walking into your meditation space is Pegasus. He is bigger than you imagined him to be, with a coat of pure snow-white and large feathered wings, similar to those of an angel. His mane is long and flowing, his eyes are a beautiful shade of violet, and his tail hangs long and straight behind him. He moves closer to you and pushes his soft velvety muzzle into your hand. In your mind you hear him speak:*

> > *Where would you go?*
> > *What would you see?*
> > *Climb on my back;*
> > *Come fly with me!*

> *You need no further invitation. You spring lightly on to Pegasus's back, your knees lodged securely behind his wings.*

> *You telepathically communicate where you would like to go and what you wish to see. As this is an astral journey, there are no limitations – you can go anywhere you wish.*

With a swish of his mighty wings, Pegasus lifts you far from your meditation area. You are flying through a midnight sky. You look down in wonder, seeing familiar streets and landmarks beneath you, but these soon fade away and you know that Pegasus is taking you to your chosen destination. You hear the sweeping sound of his wings and feel the rocking-horse motion of his back as he gallops through the night sky.

Once you reach your destination, tell Pegasus what you would like to see or learn, and enjoy all that your magical journey is showing you. Look out for symbols and signs that may carry a hidden message.

When you are ready, Pegasus begins the return flight to your home. Once again you see your house or flat below you. Pegasus descends in a magical sweep, and suddenly you find yourself back in your meditation area. You slip from the moon steed's back and spend a few moments patting him and stroking his beautiful face. As you look into his deep violet eyes, you hear him say:

> *Know that I will always be here for you, to take you where you will. Call for me by name. I will always answer.*

And with this, Pegasus fades away into his magical silvery light. The room once again darkens to the glow of your candles, and you are aware of your body and your actual surroundings once more.

- ✪ Lie still for a minute or two with your eyes closed, then slowly allow yourself to drift back to reality. Your meditation is complete.
- ✪ Blow out your candles, clear away your things and write down your meditation experiences in your Book of Earth Shadows.

The sphinx

The mysterious sphinx is said to hold all the wisdom of the universe. The sphinx is related to the griffin, and is generally depicted as having the body of a reclining lion and the head of a woman in Egyptian head gear. It is the Egyptian version of the sphinx that most people are familiar with, although the Greeks and the Babylonians also believed in this fabulous creature.

Magically speaking, the sphinx is said to have the answers to all the questions of the world, though these answers are often given in riddles and have to be worked out. The sphinx can help you to understand the art of divination and holds the mysteries of deep magic.

To question the sphinx

This spell will enable you to seek answers from the sphinx, but be warned – they may not be the ones you wish to hear. The sphinx speaks only truth, however; so whatever you think of your answer, you will do well to heed it.

What you do

⭐ Call the image of a sphinx to mind and say the following charm:

> *Circle, spiral round and round,*
> *An answer to my quest be found.*
> *Through life's spiral I will turn;*
> *The answer now I wish to learn.*

⭐ Ask your question with clarity, wording it carefully. The answer will come to you within the next few days, maybe within a dream.

The griffin

The griffin is the cousin of the sphinx. It has the head, wings and fore-claws of an eagle, and the lower body and tail of a lion. The griffin can be called upon as a guardian and protector, and also as a bringer of retribution to a wrong-doer. It represents great magic and power, and to see it in your dreams is a sign that you are protected by a higher force. With a keen sense of hearing, the griffin can teach us the art of listening to what people don't say – often the keenest insight into their lives and personality.

The griffin travels at the speed of lightning, and tradition states that there is one present within every thunderstorm. The griffin is also a symbol of the sun and links together the magical properties of Earth and Air. It is a very popular creature in heraldry and is seen in numerous coats of arms. It is sacred to the goddess Nemesis and as such can be called upon to help you deal with your own particular nemesis in your life.

To deal with your nemesis

What you do

✪ Call the image of a griffin to mind, being sure to visualise it clearly. Focus strongly on your particular nemesis and say the following spell:

Mighty griffin, I call on you and have need of you. I meet a nemesis in my life and I ask that you help me to learn this lesson and see the wisdom of its teachings. Be with me and guide me through this difficult time. Blessed be!

Centaurs

Centaurs are fantastic creatures, half horse, half man, combining all that is best in man and beast. They are the keepers of the mysteries of the heavens and, as such, they are often depicted star-gazing; thus they can be of assistance to you if you have an interest in either astrology or astronomy.

The centaur is, of course, the symbol of the zodiac sign Sagittarius. In this context it is depicted as an archer carrying a bow and arrows. The centaur rarely misses its target. It bears the gifts of healing and music, and has an in-depth knowledge of alchemy, wizardry and occult law. It is linked to the arts and can guide and inspire writers, painters, musicians and so on. It is also renowned for its ability to do battle with valour and honour.

For warrior strength

This is a great power spell to use when you feel your life has become something of a battle. We all have a warrior strength within us; it simply needs to be brought to the surface. Once you have cast this spell at your altar, you can then call on the centaur at any time simply by repeating the charm. If you memorise the charm, you will always be prepared for any challenge ahead.

What you need
A statue or picture of a centaur (this could be as simple as a picture of Sagittarius cut from a magazine), 5 pillar candles in white or neutral shades, matches or a lighter

What you do
- ✪ Take everything to the altar and light the illuminator candles. Using the pillar candles and following the instructions on page 29, cast the Circle.
- ✪ Call on the warrior strength of the centaurs in the following way:

Mighty centaur, magical steed,
Bring the warrior strength I need.
Within my life I face a foe;
True courage and bravery I will show.
Guide me through with sure-footed hooves;
I bide my time, then make my move.
Vanquish the challenges that lie ahead
That I may know peace of mind instead.
So mote it be!

To hit your target

What you need

A piece of paper, a pen, a statue of a centaur or an envelope

What you do

⭐ Write your target on the slip of paper and place it beneath the centaur statue on your altar. Alternatively, place it in the envelope. Write the word 'centaur' on the envelope and put it on your altar. Leave the target in place on your altar until you have reached it.

A quick self-blessing

If you would like to work with centaurs on a daily basis, perform this self-blessing each morning.

What you do

⭐ Look into the mirror and say the following words:

Magical centaur, steer me from strife;
May blessing bright as the stars shine within my life.
So mote it be!

Satyrs

Satyrs have the upper body of a man, and the legs, tail and cloven hooves of a goat. From their brow grows a pair of little horns, and their hair and beards are usually soft and curly. Like centaurs, they link the realms of man and beast, but satyrs have a much wilder and more untamed nature.

The most famous satyr of all is Pan, the Goat-Foot God – closely followed by Mr Tumnus of the Narnia books! Satyrs are also sacred to the gods Silvanus, Bacchus, Dionysus and Faunus. In mythology they are usually seen chasing wood nymphs and dryads through the forest, dancing with the fairies or getting intoxicated on strong wine. They are real party-goers! But satyrs are also the guardians of the woods and protectors of all wildlife. If you plan to work animal magic regularly, either at your altar or when out and about, it will benefit your rituals to have a strong link with the satyr. Bringing Pan into your home can also improve your sex life and increase the chances of conceiving a child, as he is the god of fertility and lustiness!

Attuning with the energy of Pan

The best way to attune with this god is to buy a statue and place it on your altar. Figures of satyrs and fauns can be found in garden centres, while statues of Pan himself are generally available from new age stores. If you happen to go to Greece on holiday, you will probably be able to find a statue of Pan there.

A set of panpipes could also be placed on your altar, and you could play a little tune to invoke Pan's presence. Alternatively, buy a CD of panpipe music and have this playing in the background as you work with the satyr.

Giants

This is the third time that I have taken a liberty with the word 'beasts' to include something that does not strictly fall into this category! It is true, though, that you can call upon the strength of giants in the same way that you would conjure up the strength of an animal – and if that is too lame an excuse for including them, you'll have to skip this section!

Giants are symbolic of nature in its raw and untamed state, and particular giants are often linked to particular aspects of nature, so there are mountain giants, hill giants, cave trolls, forest giants and so on. In British tradition, giants are generally seen as huge, oversized humans, carrying a club over their shoulder. They can be either benevolent (like the Welsh giant Bran the Blessed, who rescued his sister Branwen from imprisonment in Ireland) or malevolent, depending on which mythology they belong to. In other places, giants have a more animal form, for example the troll in Scandinavia, Big Foot in North America, and the Yeti or Abominable Snowman in the Himalayas.

Working with giants can help you to put things into perspective. Giants are powerful allies and protectors and can be called upon to remove any blocks within your life.

To remove blocks from your path

What you need
A tea-light and a suitable holder, matches or a lighter

What you do

⭐ Clearly visualise the image of a friendly, helpful giant in your mind. How he looks is up to you, so use your imagination. Give him a name – choose any that appeals to you.

⭐ Light the tea-light and place it in its holder, and then ask for your giant's assistance in the following way:

> *Friendly giant, swing your club;*
> *Remove all blocks from my way.*
> *Swinging, kicking, right and left,*
> *Clear my path, let no blocks stay!*

⭐ Allow the tea-light to burn down naturally. You should find that any obstacles in your way begin to disappear, leaving you free to proceed on your chosen path.

"Boulder"

Fairy godmother

A fairy godmother is not a magical beast of course, but she can certainly be used as a familiar, in the same way as any other animal.

Fairy godmothers have long been a part of childhood folklore, making wishes and dreams come true. They are the epitome of elemental magic and continue to capture our imagination, regardless of our age or maturity. However much we may laugh at ourselves for it, a part of us remains entranced by the idea of the fairy godmother, and it is deeply ingrained into our psyche that if only we can find her and make contact with her, life will be perfect. Well, maybe not perfect, but certainly more magical.

So why does this character from children's fiction refuse to leave our consciousness when we enter the world of adulthood? Because she is the Great Goddess in disguise! – a representation of the feminine in nature. We can call upon her to realise our dreams and fill our lives with magic.

To have a boon granted

Before you perform this spell, reacquaint yourself with the magic of fairy tales. Re-read *Cinderella*, watch *The Wizard of Oz*, do whatever you need to do to bring the concept of the fairy godmother freshly into your mind. Talking to a small child can help you to recapture your own childhood response to the fairy godmother.

Before you work this spell, make sure that the boon you wish to have granted is the true desire of your heart.

What you need
A silver candle, matches or a lighter

What you do
✪ Light the silver candle, close your eyes and visualise your own fairy godmother standing before you. Her wings are large and sparkly, and her wand is upraised, ready to grant your boon. When you can see her clearly, recite the following charm three times:

Fairy Godmother, wand held high,
Keeper of my dreams,
I acknowledge your presence within my life,
For nothing is what it seems.
Fiction, fable, myth and legend –
But I see through your disguise.
Magic did not with childhood end;
The Goddess stands before my eyes.
Shining star-light in your wings,
Your gown shimmers like the moon.
Join me in my magical ring;
Fey-Mother, grant my boon!

✪ Make your wish, blowing out the candle as you do so. Save the candle for repeating this spell for future boons. Spend the rest of the day doing something 'fey' – read a fairy tale, work magic to call your true prince/princess, dust your collection of fairies and unicorns or consult the Faery Oracle cards if you have a pack. Watch out for signs that your fairy godmother has granted your wish, and thank her when your spell manifests.

Here be Dragons

What better way to end this book of magical beasts than with the most magical beast of all – the dragon! As timeless creatures of ancient power, strength and wisdom, dragons appeal to all ages and both sexes. While unicorns and mermaids may have a somewhat 'girlie' appeal, dragons are embraced by men and women alike, and while it is still considered by some a little childish to like fairies, it is undoubtedly 'cool' to love dragons! They are exceedingly popular, and their magic transcends age and social culture. Dragons have been associated with leather-jacketed bikers and long-haired heavy rockers – in fact a whole collection of figures featuring dragons riding Harleys and playing drums and keyboards has been created to capture this market! At the other end of the scale, cute baby dragons wearing nappies are sold to children and young ladies, while Norbert has become something of a legend in his own right among Harry Potter fans!

So what is it about dragons that makes them so relevant to the modern world? Well, maybe it's that dragons have seemingly been around forever. All cultures, the world over, have legends and tales of dragons. Dragons have never really gone away. The old tales have been retold to younger generations time and time again, for who does not know the legend of St George and the Dragon or that Oriental dragons are said to bring good luck?

In this chapter we will explore various techniques of dragon magic, including how to use their energies to cast a Circle and call the quarters. But first, let's take a closer look at dragons themselves.

Dragons of Earth

The element of Earth is associated with the north quarter of the Circle. The dragons of this element come in shades of green and occasionally brown. They are linked to mountains, hills, moors and forests; to the depths of winter; and to the witching hour of midnight. Earth dragons are the easiest to invoke, as they have such a close connection to our world and are never really far away. A dragon bowl (available from occult stores) filled with rock salt can be used to represent Earth dragons during ritual. They are reasonably friendly and will work willingly as familiars, assisting in magic for fertility, stability, prosperity, career, pets and home.

Dragons of Air

Dragons of Air are associated with the eastern quarter of the Circle. They appear in shades of yellow, gold and saffron, and are associated with the winds and clouds, the season of spring, and the magical hour of dawn. Air dragons are the most elusive and can be difficult to work with by themselves. However, they will assist in rituals with other dragons present, and their energies can be directed towards creativity, inspiration, examinations and tests, clarity of thought and so on. A stick or cone of sweet-smelling incense set in a dragon-shaped incense burner can represent the dragons of Air during ritual.

Dragons of Fire

Fire dragons can be tricky, so be careful! Always state your need for non-destructive Fire energies when calling this dragon, and turn down the heating! Fire dragons are associated with the southern quarter of the Circle. The energies that surround them are hot and can be used in spells of love, passion, protection and sexual energy. They are linked to deserts and volcanoes, to the season of summer and to the heat of the noonday sun. Fire dragons are the strongest form of dragon protection; they will work tirelessly to keep their charges safe. They are red or orange in colour and can help to remove blocks or negativity from your life. A dragon-shaped candlestick, preferably red or orange, can be used to represent Fire dragons in your rituals.

Dragons of Water

Water dragons are the gentlest of all the dragons and make excellent personal familiars, particularly if you live near the sea or a large body of water such as a loch or lake. They vary in colour from the deepest indigo blues, through paler blues, to turquoise and aquamarine. Their wings are much smaller and their bodies more serpentine than those of their fellow dragons. Water dragons are associated with the western quarter of the Circle and are, of course, linked to oceans, rivers, lochs, lakes and streams, as well as to the damp season of autumn and the hour of dusk. They are also associated with rainfall, working closely with the Air dragons to bring about downpours! Magically speaking, Water dragons can assist with all magic of divination, psychic ability, dreams, emotions and healing. A dragon bowl filled with water can be used to represent Water dragons during ritual.

Ice and snow dragons

As you may have guessed, these dragons are associated with Arctic regions, snow-capped mountains, glaciers and ice caverns. They are white and silver in colour, having a truly sparkling appearance with eyes of an icy blue. Their scales often have a snowflake pattern, and their spines resemble icicles. Ice and snow dragons can be called upon to freeze a situation and thus they are great companions in binding spells. If you have a strong affinity with the realm of winter, as I do, an ice and snow dragon could become your main familiar. They can be represented in ritual by a picture or statue. Never try to work with ice and snow dragons and fire dragons at the same time, as their energies are in complete opposition.

Chaos dragons

Chaos dragons come in shades of black, pewter, dark grey and deepest purple. They represent the negative energies that keep the universe in balance. They can be quite frightening in appearance, with large leathery wings and a viciously barbed tail. They can be called upon to remove negative people, destructive relationships and bad habits from your life. They will go direct to the source of the problem, so be sure that this isn't you before you call them! Chaos dragons have their uses, and skilled practitioners may call on them when in need, but they should never be used as personal familiars and power animals, unless you want to fill your life with chaos. They are, however, the best guys to call on to undo magic. We'll be looking at this a little later.

Creating a dragon altar

If you are going to work with dragons regularly, I strongly recommend that you put together a full working altar dedicated to them. The sooner you begin this, the better, as such an altar will take you a while to set up. Most altars are put together over a period of months or even years, so don't worry if you can't get everything together in one go. You can easily improvise with household utensils in the meantime. Never wait until you have the perfect set of magical tools before you work magic, or the chances are you'll never cast a spell!

Because it's an altar, not a shrine, your dragon altar will include ritual tools such as an athame (for inscribing), a pentacle (for charging objects with magical energy) a wand (for casting the Circle and directing magical energies) and a chalice (for containing any liquid you may need for your rituals). Your altar should have a large working surface and should preferably be made of wood or glass. If you want to use an altar cloth, try to find one with a dragon design. Over the altar you might like to hang a large elaborate mirror to represent the doorway into the astral realm and shadow world beyond. Place statues and figures of dragons on your altar and add the dragon bowl filled with rock salt, the incense in a dragon-shaped burner, the candle in a dragon-shaped holder and the dragon bowl of water mentioned above to represent the four elemental dragons of Earth, Air, Fire and Water.

HERE BE DRAGONS

Add two illuminator candles in dragon-style candleholders.

Your dragon altar will be personal to you, so if you wish to work with ice and snow dragons, add an appropriate figure. However, I don't recommend a chaos dragon for a magical altar! Other items you might like to include are dragon stones (similar to rune stones), dragon tarot cards (perhaps in a box engraved with dragons), a pewter or silver dragon pendant, a crystal ball on a dragon-style stand and a dragon-headed ritual staff. Collect whatever objects you like, but don't forget to leave enough space on your altar for you to work.

Once you have set up a dragon altar, you will find that it exudes a magic of its own and really enhances your living space. I love my dragon altar and work there regularly. I find that it is something of a talking point too – everyone who visits my house for the first time comments on the dragons!

A dragon Circle-casting

Before you begin to work rituals of dragon magic you should always cast a Circle. This particular Circle-casting has been created specifically for working with dragons as familiars – and it can also be used as a protection spell when you are going out and about. The basic idea is to surround yourself entirely with dragon energy.

What you need
Your athame (if you have one), your dragon staff (if you have one)

What you do

✪ Stand in the centre of your ritual space, close your eyes and say:

> *Out of the darkness comes the mighty dragon. Magical companion, wise counsellor, protector and friend, I bid thee welcome.*

✪ Visualise the shadowy shape of a dragon moving into your space, then chant the following Circle casting nine times as you turn in a circle with your athame (or your finger, if you don't have an athame) outstretched before you:

> *Dragon, breathe your fire round and round;*
> *By dragon's breath I'm safe and sound.*

⊙ Visualise a ring of dragon fire and smoke surrounding you and illuminating you in a magical light. Tap your dragon staff on the floor three times (or stamp your foot if you don't have a staff) and say:

> *By dragon power, I declare this magical Circle sealed.*

⊙ To release the Circle at the end of the ritual, simply say:

> *The dragon power of this Circle is released. Blessed be!*

Dragon quarter calls

A pretty way to enhance this ritual is to invest in tea-light holders fashioned to look like dragons of the relevant elemental colour. Place them at the appropriate cardinal points (north, south, east and west) of your Circle and use tea-lights instead of candles for the following calls.

What you need

1 green, 1 red, 1 yellow and 1 blue candle, with appropriate holders; matches or a lighter

What you do

⊙ Face the northern point of the Circle, raise your arms high in invocation and say:

> *Dragon of earth, dragon of land,*
> *Dragon power come to my hand!*
> Light a green candle in the north.

⊙ Face the eastern point of the Circle, raise your arms high in invocation and say:

> *Dragon of air, dragon of smoke,*
> *Dragon power I do invoke.*

Light a yellow candle in the east.

⭐ Face the southern point of the Circle, raise your arms high in invocation and say:

> *Dragon of flame, dragon of non-destructive fire,*
> *Dragon power, fulfil my desire.*

Light a red candle in the south

⭐ Face the western point of the Circle, raise your arms high in invocation and say:

> *Dragon of water, dragon of sea,*
> *Dragon power come unto me!*

Light a blue candle in the west.

⭐ To release the dragon energies after your ritual, go round the Circle widdershins (anti-clockwise), snuffing out each candle and saying:

> *Mighty dragon, I give you thanks and release you. Blessed be!*

To reverse a spell

Occasionally you may fall into the trap of casting a spell and later on wishing you hadn't! Most new witches make this mistake – we've all been there, so don't panic! The trick is ... more magic, in the form of a reversal spell.

When it comes to reversing magic you can't beat the power of a chaos dragon! He will put a stop to any magical mess you may have landed yourself in! Being a chaos dragon, he will create some fall-out, but this should be minimal, as you have taken responsibility for your mistake and are doing something about it.

What you need

Your athame (if you have one), your dragon staff (if you have one), a piece of paper, a black pen, a black candle, matches or a lighter, your cauldron or a heatproof dish

What you do

- ⊛ Using your athame and staff, perform the dragon Circle-casting as described on page 171.
- ⊛ Using the black pen, write the spell that you originally cast on the piece of paper. Roll it up into a scroll.
- ⊛ Light the black candle and call the dragon in the following way:

> *Great Chaos Dragon,*
> *Bring your power to me.*
> *Reverse this magic!*
> *Let it be!*

- ⊛ Light the spell paper in the candle's flame and allow it to burn in your cauldron or the heatproof dish.
- ⊛ Snuff out the candle and allow the dragon to do his work.

For protection in great need

If you find yourself in a sticky spot and require protection urgently, try this quick spell.

What you do

- ⊛ Visualise a huge, bright red Fire dragon, breathing flames of fire and brimstone! When you can see him clearly in your mind, begin to chant the following spell, either out loud or in your head. Continue until you reach home or a place of safety, or until the danger has passed.

> *Firestarter! Firestarter! Firestarter!*
> *Protect me! Protect me! Protect me!*

- ⊛ Once you are sure you are safe, thank your guardian and release him.

To empower a dragon charm

For constant dragon protection, buy a charm or pendant fashioned to look like a dragon. There are many of these available so take your time and choose one that you really love.

What you need
Matches or a lighter, your charm

What you do

⭐ Take the charm to your dragon altar and light the candles.

⭐ Holding the charm between your palms, envisage a strong white light entering it from your hands – this is known as empowering an object. As you do so, close your eyes and chant the following words for as long as you remain focused:

May the Dragon of Protection be with me always.

⭐ Wear the pendant at all times and re-empower it every six months.

Treasure worm

In the tale of the hero-king Beowulf, the treasure worm was a leg-less serpent-like dragon who guarded a huge treasure trove. Beowulf found this treasure, and, being king, he wrongly assumed that it belonged to him and carried it off to his castle! In retribution the treasure worm laid waste to Beowulf's kingdom, breathing fire on all in its path and eventually slaying King Beowulf himself. The moral of the tale? Never steal a dragon's treasure, as they are very partial to sparkling gems and pretty trinkets!

If you have valuables in your home that you would like to protect from thieves, use this spell to invoke a treasure worm to guard them for you.

What you need
A list of all the items you want the treasure worm to guard, matches or a lighter

What you do

⊙ Take the list of items to your dragon altar and light the candles. Say the following spell three times:

> *Treasure Worm, guard these things*
> *And vanquish any thieves.*
> *Hide my treasure beneath your wings*
> *Until my property I do retrieve.*
> *So mote it be!*

⊙ Leave the list on your altar and blow out the candles.

Retribution of the wyvern

The wyvern is cousin to the dragon and he is very aggressive! He is a symbol of punishment, karma and retribution, and he can be called upon to punish any who would do you harm. But be warned, the wyvern is the indiscriminate distributor of retribution, so make sure your own slate is clean before you call him!

What you need
Your athame (if you have one), your dragon staff (if you have one), some black candles, matches or a lighter

What you do

⊛   Using your athame and staff, perform the dragon Circle-casting as described on page 171. Light the black candles and say the following spell:

>   *Vicious Wyvern, find my foe;*
>   *Make him see and let him know*
>   *That if he wish me harm and woe*
>   *Your fiery breath will cast its glow*
>   *And retribution he shall know!*

⊛   Allow the candle to burn down naturally (for safety's sake remain in the room while this is happening) and wait for the spell to play itself out in your life.

The Charm of Making

Much has been written about the infamous Charm of Making – much of it exaggerated and distorted. As a result, this charm is shrouded in mystery and power. So what exactly is it? The Charm of Making is simply a manifestation chant that utilises dragon power. It gives added strength to your spells and – if you use it wisely, only when you have a true need – it can make manifestation occur more quickly.

What you do

⭐ At the end of your spell-casting, speak the following words:

> *By dragon's strength and dragon's light,*
> *These words are sent with power and might.*
> *Hear now the Charm of Making,*
> *Sacred magic undertaking.*
> *Through Earth, Air, Water, Fire,*
> *Manifest what I desire.*
> *By dragon's strength and dragon's light,*
> *By dragon power this spell is right!*

⭐ Remember that if you are greedy and use this spell too often, the dragon power will desert you.

Afterword

I n the pages of this book I have woven together some of the natural history, folklore, mythology, literature, magic and witchcraft of animals. The animal kingdom is so vast, however, that here we have only just touched the tip of the iceberg. I hope that my words have been enough to whet your appetite and that you will continue to study animal magic and will go on to create your own spells and rituals using those in this book as a guideline.

My final words to you must be with regard to animal welfare. As I have worked my way through this book, I have tried to dispel many of the myths and prejudices that result in much animal suffering, and reveal instead the true beauty of the creature behind the superstition. The animal kingdom has been on the receiving end of much cruelty by humankind. My goal has been to show animals in a new light, as magical beings in their own right and, above all, as our equals.

If I could make one wish it would be this: that everyone who reads this book begins to view themselves as a champion of the animal kingdom. If more individuals would stand up for the rights of our fellow creatures, the bottom would fall out of the fur and ivory trades, fewer species would be on the endangered list, there would be little demand for illegally owned exotic pets, and the shelters that are now filled to bursting point with unwanted pets would be empty. Stand up and be counted. Bat for their team and your magical familiars will reward you tenfold for your allegiance!

I would also like to take this opportunity to thank all of you who have taken the time to write to me over the past two or three years. I love hearing from my readers and I am grateful for all of your support – so thank you!

Finally, remember that although magic and witchcraft should be taken seriously, they should also be fun! Don't be afraid to experiment with your own spells and have fun with your castings. May your life be filled with magic!

Farewell, Earth Child, until our next merry meeting!

Blessed be!

Morgana

Animal Attributes

Animals of this world

Animal	Magical characteristics	Divinities
Badger	family loyalty, bravery, warrior spirit	Herne
Bat	voluntary isolation, new perspectives, avoiding obstacles	Hades, Hecate, Persephone
Bear	the wisdom of ancestors, true paths, decisions	Arduinna, Artemis, Arthur, Atalanta
Bee	centre of attention	Aphrodite, Demeter
Cat	freedom, independence, mystery, subtlety, stealth	Artemis, Bast, the Cailleach, Diana, Freya, Isis, Liberty
Crow	darkness, battle strength, the Otherworld	the Morrigan
Deer/stag	strength, grace, otherworldliness, power, majesty, humility	Apollo, Arawn, Artemis, Britomart, Diana, Herne, Nemesis
Dolphin	fun, playfulness, balance, healing	Apollo, Aphrodite, Dionysus, Eros, Neptune, Thetis, Venus
Dove	love, peace, harmony	Aphrodite, Venus
Elephant	gentleness, family loyalty, removal of obstacles	Ganesha
Fish	abundance, prosperity	Aphrodite, Isis, Kuan Yin, Neptune, Poseidon
Fox	slinkiness, sexuality, slyness	Aphrodite, Artemis, Diana
Frog	sexuality, lust, loss of virginity, rebirth, initiation	Aphrodite, Hecate, Isis, Venus
Hare	divination, moon magic, joy	Aphrodite, Cupid, Diana, Eostre, Eros, Hecate, Venus

Animal	Magical characteristics	Divinities
Hedgehog	prickliness and protection	the faeries
Horse	royalty, nobility, strength, stamina, valour	Epona, Helios, Mars, Poseidon, Rhiannon
Magpie	divination	the Morrigan
Mole	seeing the light, getting to the bottom of things	Hades, Persephone
Mouse	inconspicuousness	Apollo
Owl	night, winter, old age, death and rebirth, wisdom	Athene, the Cailleach, Guinevere, Hecate
Peacock	self-confidence, vanity, protection against intruders	Hera, Isis, Lakshmi, Sarasvati
Rabbit	fertility, good	Eostre
Rat	intelligence, agility, resilience	Persephone
Raven	guardianship	the Morrigan
Robin	winter and the winter solstice	Thor
Sea horse	grace, beauty, going with the flow, seduction, sexuality	Aphrodite, Neptune, Poseidon
Seal	separation, romantic break-up	Aphrodite, Neptune, Poseidon
Snake	wisdom, sexuality, sensuality, immortality, reincarnation, guardianship	Apollo, Astarte, Bast, Boreas, Conall, Cuchulain, Demeter, Fionn, Gaia, Isis, Medusa, Nimue, Vivienne, Zeus
Squirrel	saving and hoarding	Thor
Swan	beauty, grace	Aphrodite, Apollo, Merlin, Morgan la Fey, the Valkyries, Venus, Zeus
Toad	witchcraft skills, psychic abilities	Circe, Hecate
Whale	balance, relaxation, slowness	Gaia, Neptune, Poseidon
Wolf/dog	strength, stamina, loyalty, protection	Hecate, Mars, Merlin, the Morrigan

Animals of the Otherworld

Animal	Magical characteristics	Divinities
Centaur	astrology, astronomy, arts, knowledge, valour, honour	Jupiter
Dragon	power, protection	Arthur, Merlin, Odin
Fairy godmother	granting of wishes	the Great Goddess
Giant	perspective, alliance and protection, removal of blocks	Bran, Odin
Griffin	the unspoken, speed, retribution	Nemesis
Mermaid/siren	love, seduction, creativity, inspiration	Aphrodite, Neptune, Poseidon, Venus
Phoenix	rebirth, reincarnation, passion	Osiris, Ra
Satyr	fertility, lust, wine	Bacchus, Dionysus, Faunus, Pan, Silvanus
Selkie	See 'Seal' above	
Sphinx	answers and riddles, divination, deep magic	Isis
Unicorn	magic, enchantment, speed, beauty, chastity, virginity, valour	Epona, the faeries, Guinevere, Rhiannon
Vampire	the darker side	Hades, Persephone
Winged horse	escape, new heights, inspiration, meditation, poetry	Epona, Rhiannon, the Sylphs of Air

Index

Diem mail raise